Laboratory Manager's Professional Reference

This book was printed with acid-free recycled content paper containing **10% POSTCONSUMER WASTE**

HOLT, RINEHART AND WINSTON
A Harcourt Education Company

Austin • New York • Orlando • Atlanta • San Francisco • Boston • Dallas • Toronto • London

DISCLAIMER

The content of this manual is intended for informational purposes only and not as a substitute for legal and other professional advice. Ongoing research discoveries, experience, and new legislation may affect the information contained in this manual. Circumstances are also significant in evaluating and determining an appropriate course of action. Readers are encouraged to consult pertinent local, state, and federal laws, legal counsel, other relevant professionals, and reports on recent developments. No warranty, guarantee, or representation of any kind is made by the publisher or the editor as to the accuracy or sufficiency of the information discussed in this manual. Therefore, readers should not assume that all necessary precautionary measures are presented in this manual and that other or additional information or measures may not be required. Neither the publisher nor the editor assumes any liability for any loss, injury, and/or damage to persons or property arising from this manual.

Cover: HRW Photo by Sam Dudgeon

Printed in the United States of America

ISBN 0-03-064921-8

3 4 5 6 7 862 07 06 05 04 03

Table of Contents

Table of Contents, continued

HAZARDS AND RISK MANAGEMENT

Why do you need risk management?

Whether we realize it or not, we are all exposed to risk on a daily basis. Taking a shower in the morning, driving our cars, cooking our food, and mowing our lawns all expose us to varying degrees of risk. If we really thought about the risks we take every day, we would probably never leave our beds. Yet we cope with risks somehow. How do we decide which risks we'll take?

Daily risk versus risk in the science classroom

In daily life, we decide unconsciously to expose ourselves to particular risks. The decision is typically based on a variety of factors from our own experiences. Not all of these factors may be completely rational. However, this risk-management system seems to work rather well for our daily living.

Risk management in the science classroom is similar to that of daily living. Hands-on activities, demonstrations, student interactions, and experiences outside the four walls of the school are valid and essential methods of enhancing the learning experience. All of these methods also contain some degree of risk. But when students' eyes light up in understanding, the value of such activities is obvious.

Risk can be a good thing

Our focus so far has been on the negative aspects of risk. Forgetting that risk can have positive outcomes as well, depending on how we choose to deal with risk, is easy. We can try to avoid risk by only lecturing to bored students, or we can try to make the educational process as vibrant as possible by carefully choosing which risks to take. The trick is to establish some degree of balance when dealing with risk. This balance should reflect your personal feelings about risk. Helping you establish this balance is one of the goals of this book.

Another goal of this book is to help you develop a formal, conscious mechanism for assessing risk. That way, you will not expose students (or yourself) to unnecessary levels of risk. An important first step is to analyze some common conceptions (and misconceptions) about risk. You need to be ready to deal with these ideas as you work with your colleagues and your school's administration.

What conceptions of risk must you face?

Humans have been exposed to risk throughout history. However, our farming and hunting ancestors seldom were concerned with risk— at least not in a formal sense. Common sense or trial-and-error methods of assessing risk prevailed over more-analytical means. Even as people began working in factories, no one was developing systematic ways to avoid risk. Why has risk come to play a more prominent part in our lives only in modern times?

The advances of science and technology has contributed significantly to the public's increasing awareness of and concern about risk. As the world has become more complex, so have the risks that people face on a regular basis. This increase in complexity means that it is harder to understand how equipment works and hence what risks may be inherent in its use.

 **SAFETY INFORMATION**

Much has been written about the misconceptions of risk. A book entitled *Taking Risks: The Management of Uncertainty,* by K. MacCrimmon and D. Wehrung, and an article from *The New York Times,* "Hidden Rules Often Distort Ideas of Risk," by D. Goleman, are two informative references.

Several factors may distort judgments about risk

Limited understanding of the various existing technologies leads people to attribute far greater risk to certain activities than actually exists. Researchers have identified the following reasons that people may believe that risks of a given activity are unacceptable.

❑ Imposed risks are perceived as more hazardous than risks that are assumed voluntarily.

❑ Risks that provide more benefit to others than to us seem more hazardous than risks that provide more benefit to us than to others.

❑ Uncontrollable risks are perceived as more hazardous than those in which we have some personal control.

❑ Human-made risks are believed to be more hazardous than natural risks.

❑ Risks associated with catastrophic events seem more frightening than risks associated with daily events.

❑ Risks associated with unfamiliar technologies are considered more hazardous than risks associated with common technologies.

❑ A risk that has been heavily covered in the media seems far more hazardous than may be justifiable based on fact.

Moreover, if experts in a particular field dismiss risk-related concerns, regardless of whether such a dismissal is based on scientific evidence, the usual effect is to create distrust and anger in the public's mind.

Why we tend to ignore risk

Recognizing and understanding the risks for students, teachers, and other school staff are extremely important. Yet this sort of examination of a school's curricula is very rare. Many excuses about why risk is ignored are made, but most fail to account for the causes of accidents. Check to see if you or your school is guilty of one of these attitudes:

✔ **Complacency** If there have been no dangerous incidents involving something we do or were taught, we may believe the activity is safe even if it is not.

✔ **Lack of time** Hazard assessments of school activities are often low on the teacher's to-do list because of daily pressures and packed schedules.

✔ **Fear of complexity** Traditionally, risk assessments have been formal processes carried out by well-trained individuals using extensive data. Such assessments were not commonly performed outside insurance or industrial circles.

✔ **Rationalization** A common tendency is to assume that if students prepare for the upcoming activity, nothing will go wrong. In case of an accident, the blame may fall upon a student, which allows us to avoid admitting the hazards in our activities.

✔ **Wait-and-see** Some teachers feel that correcting problems only when necessary is sufficient risk management.

✔ **Fatalism** Lastly, some teachers take the approach that accidents are inevitable, regardless of planning and prevention efforts.

 SAFETY SUGGESTIONS

How This Book Helps You Fight These Attitudes

Complacency You can use this book as a resource to remind yourself and others about the need for regular risk management.

Lack of time This book is organized to make risk management easier for you to handle.

Fear of complexity This book explains risk management as a simple step-by-step method that is easy to implement.

Rationalization This book combats the misconception that the teacher has no responsibility for risk management. (See the chapter entitled "Legal Issues.")

Wait-and-see This book focuses on meaningful, easy-to-implement prevention techniques.

Fatalism This book clearly explains how to manage the many safety factors that are within your control.

The basic causes of accidents

The attitudes described above are certainly not prudent and may even be reckless. An implicit assumption in the excuses for ignoring risk is that dealing constructively with risk is beyond the duties of teachers or the resources made available to teachers.

However, a quick look at the most common causes of accidents reveals that many of the causes are firmly within the duties of a teacher. Even those causes not thoroughly within a teacher's control can be strongly affected by a teacher's guidance. Examples of common causes of accidents that are within the teacher's control include the

❑ failure to perform inspections or to give adequate instruction

 SAFETY INFORMATION

For more on the legal duties of a teacher, see the chapter "Legal Issues."

❑ failure to properly plan or conduct the activity

❑ failure to properly design, construct, or lay out the activity

❑ failure to provide protective devices, equipment, or tools

❑ failure to use the provided protective devices, equipment, or tools

❑ failure to follow safety rules or instructions

❑ failure to allow for a disability

❑ lack of knowledge or poor mental attitude

❑ use of defective equipment (either knowingly or unknowingly)

 SAFETY INFORMATION

This list of common causes of accidents is taken from *CRC Handbook of Laboratory Safety,* 2nd Edition, by Norman Steere. See the appendix for more information.

Why you can't afford to ignore risk

Years ago, students had few inhibitions or concerns about their classroom activities—students were willing to do whatever they were told. Parents usually took the view that teachers were the experts—teachers were considered to know what they were doing and were trusted to not expose children to risk. Many of these attitudes have changed in recent years. Parents (and their children) are now much more willing to question teachers and school districts about school curricula and the abilities of teachers in the classroom.

Even if some teachers use excuses to try to avoid their duties to provide the most effective and safest possible educational experience for students, these teachers will likely be held accountable for their responsibilities sooner or later, whether by their administration, their students, or the parents of their students. You'll be better able to meet the challenges of having a safe classroom if you are familiar with risk, know what techniques to use to deal with it, and are aware of the many factors that affect the public's perceptions of risk.

A short course on the theory of risk management

What is risk management anyway? A good first step in answering this question is to get some terminology straight. In common speech, the terms *risk, hazard,* and *accident* are often treated synonymously. Actually, they each have specific meanings for serious students of risk management.

Risk management 101: Terminology (What is risk anyway?)

One approach to defining risk is described below:

A totally inclusive definition of risk includes hazards, dangers, potential for loss, the degree or probability of a specific exposure for loss as well as the liability to injury, damage, loss or pain. It encompasses jeopardy or the exposure to extreme danger for any situation. Events with both chance and voluntary provocation are included. Loss potential due to risk also embraces rational behavior, irrational behavior, natural phenomena, and any other potential for realizing unwanted, negative consequences of any event. (Vernon Grose, *Managing Risk: Systematic Loss Prevention for Executives,* [Englewood Cliffs: Prentice Hall, Inc., 1987] 24)

A simpler definition of **risk** is shown in the margin. The definition of **hazard** indicates that *risk* is due to *hazards*. When hazards do cause harm, an **accident** can occur. For this reason, although this book as a whole concerns itself with *risk* management, many of the chapters focus on different *hazards*.

 **DEFINITIONS**

risk
the likelihood and extent of harm or loss

hazard
any real or potential condition that can cause harm

accident
an unplanned, occasional, but foreseeable and hazardous consequence of an unsafe act

Risk management 102: Predictions (Methods of the scientist)

To anticipate risk is to try to predict or to "see into the future." Yet we cannot possibly anticipate every risk in every situation. Some complex situations would require an unreasonable amount of time for such an analysis. Also, we cannot anticipate how each and every rational person will behave, let alone how an irrational person might act. Finally, even if a procedure as a whole does not seem risky, one of the steps involved may have hazards that pose risks.

Despite these very real obstacles to risk management, here's a simple approach you can use to overcome these obstacles and to manage the aspects of the activity that are under your control. Because you are a science teacher, the methods for prediction should be very familiar to you. They are the same ones used by scientists to investigate any scientific problem!

❑ **Analysis**—separating an activity into its constituent elements and then understanding why the activity works the way it does and what hazards and risks may be involved (Analysis can be done using physical methods [taking something apart] or cognitive methods [examining a diagram]).

❑ **Synthesis**—identifying the hazards and associated risks each step of an activity

❑ **Simulation**—producing an alternate form of reality that approximates the real activity but without the associated hazards (Simulations can be computerized or noncomputerized.

An important caveat is that the simulation must not be so far divorced from the actual activity that hazards are no longer conceivable.)

❑ **Testing**—performing a "dry run" of the activity

Note that these methods need not be used in isolation. They can be (and often should be) used in combination.

Risk management 103: Taxonomy (What risks to look for)

In general, there are two types of risk: **static** and **dynamic.** Static risks are well established and easy to identify. When spotting static risks by using your prediction skills, check the following sources of information:

✔ personal knowledge or experience

✔ checklists

✔ reviews of policies, procedures, and instruction manuals

✔ reference books and federal, state, and local standards, regulations, and laws

DEFINITIONS

static risks
easily predictable risks that are easily verifiable

dynamic risks
difficult-to-predict risks that arise from changing situations and human fallibility

Although dynamic risks are much harder to identify, many of them can be discovered during the prediction process. Here are ways to remain aware of dynamic risks when making predictions:

✔ Anticipate what might go wrong in a given situation.

✔ Maintain a good working knowledge of the activity.

✔ Analyze creatively the risk of the activity.

Like a good chess player, you will often need to consider the future consequences of an action at an early point in an activity.

Risk management 104: Methodology (How to deal with what you find)

Once you've looked for static and dynamic risks by using your prediction skills, you may want to implement one or more of the five commonly accepted methods for dealing with risk:

❑ **Acceptance** At times, you may knowingly accept some amount of risk, given the nature of science education. The difficulty of this aspect of risk management is in deciding how much risk is acceptable and how to balance it against the pedagogic value of the activity. There will always be an element of risk. However, a careful evaluation of the foreseeable risks may minimize the unforeseeable risks.

❑ **Reduction** If possible, the best way to handle risk is to reduce risk. A less hazardous alternative to an apparatus may be used, or some other alteration may be made to an activity. Classroom controls that address student behaviors may be implemented.

❑ **Avoidance** Because completely avoiding risk in science teaching is impossible, this method is less fruitful than the other methods. Occasionally, finding an alternative activity that does not have the number of hazards of the original activity is possible. But beware of "substitution of risk"—while avoiding one risk, you may introduce another.

❑ **Dilution** Using this method, you recognize that an identified risk will be present at some point in the activity no matter what actions are taken, and you make adjustments to minimize the risk. For example, an activity may be divided into segments so that you better manage the hazardous portions of the activity.

❑ **Transference** This approach involves having other people assume some of the risk. This method is of limited practical use to teachers. Transference is usually accomplished by means of insurance, typically an expensive proposition. Insurance should be thought of as a supplemental means of reducing risk rather than as a substitute for responsibility. Direct steps to reduce risks in the curriculum are still necessary.

Now that you've completed the short course on the theory of risk management, you are ready for the next chapter. The next chapter details a step-by-step approach you can use to assess individual hazards in activities that you and your students do.

 SAFETY SUGGESTIONS

Note that if an activity is hazardous enough to warrant the "Dilution" approach, that activity should probably not be a part of the curriculum unless it has an extremely high pedagogic value.

SAFETY INFORMATION

This analysis of how to deal with risk is based on the principles set forth in Vernon Grose's book *Managing Risk: Systematic Loss Prevention for Executives* (see especially p. 47). See the appendix of this book for more information.

A BASIC HAZARD ASSESSMENT METHOD

Overview of the process

In the past, formal assessments of hazards were time consuming and complicated. As a result, few teachers performed them. But the process below is a streamlined step-by-step approach that builds on some strategies you already use as a teacher. You can use this approach to analyze a specific experiment or activity in terms of hazards.

Each of the following steps will be explained in further detail later in this chapter.

- ✔ Identify the hazards of an activity.

- ✔ Evaluate the identified hazards.

- ✔ Select appropriate controls for the hazards.

- ✔ Implement and apply the selected controls to the activity.

- ✔ Review the hazards of an activity periodically, and make needed adjustments to the activity.

 SAFETY INFORMATION

Common complaints

"Why is this process only qualitative?"
Unfortunately, data on accidents in instructional laboratories are hard to come by and mainly anecdotal. This process can easily be made quantitative if such data become available.

"Why does the process seem so time consuming?"
Any process seems time consuming at first, but with practice the process becomes easier. This hazard assessment method can quickly become an automatic part of any teacher's repertoire.

1. Identify the hazards

The goal of identifying hazards is to create a list of every hazard possible for a given activity. Every hazard, no matter how trivial or unlikely it may seem, should be included. Admittedly, there is no way to make a complete list, so just do your best.

 SAFETY INFORMATION

To see this process implemented for the classic "Specific Heat of Metals" laboratory experiment, turn to p. 13.

Role-playing: The naïve student versus the well-informed expert

Having the proper mindset when creating the hazard list is important. This mindset must allow for two different viewpoints to be considered. Potential hazards to both students and teachers must be identified, so thinking like students who have little or no experience in science is important. What seems obvious to teachers who are experts in their fields may seem very unclear to students. An open, unbiased attitude toward hazards in the classroom is essential.

What are the hazards?

Hazards are categorized in a variety of ways. Here's one set of categories:

- ❑ **physical hazards**—associated with an object or apparatus

 SAFETY SUGGESTIONS

The team approach

Simultaneously maintaining the differing viewpoints of the expert and the student is a tricky balancing act. Try using a team approach, possibly even including one or two students during the assessment. When various degrees of experience and expertise are involved, better and more ideas are generated, resulting in a better analysis.

❑ **mechanical hazards**—associated with the operation of an object or apparatus

❑ **chemical hazards**—associated with specific chemicals

❑ **noise hazards**—associated with loud sounds that occur over a short period of time or low-intensity, continuous sounds

❑ **electrical hazards**—associated with bad electrical wiring or poor setup of the experiment

❑ **thermal hazards**—associated with apparatus that cause burns or other forms of heat damage

❑ **radiation hazards**—associated with either ionizing radiation, which can damage cells directly, or nonionizing radiation, which affects tissues or organs through the absorption of energy

❑ **pressure hazards**—associated with vacuums or high pressures

❑ **biological hazards**—associated with exposure to specimens, tissues, cultures, or body fluids

> **SAFETY INFORMATION**
>
> These categories are further addressed in other chapters in this book.

2. Evaluate the hazards

Evaluation of hazards requires assessment of both the risk levels of the hazards in an activity and prioritization of the specific hazards involved.

Risk-level analysis

As discussed earlier, the key to determining if an activity is appropriate for your classroom is to distinguish between acceptable and unacceptable levels of risk. The following questions may aid in this task.

✔ What levels of risk are associated with the hazards in this activity?

✔ What is the pedagogic advantage of this activity?

✔ Does the overall level of risk of the activity outweigh the pedagogic benefits of the activity?

The decision square in the following figure provides a qualitative structure to help you decide if an activity is worth the risks that the activity presents. If the overall level of risk is greater than the pedagogic value of an activity, then that activity should be eliminated from your lesson plans.

<table>
<tr><td>High Pedagogy
Low Risk</td><td>High Pedagogy
High Risk</td></tr>
<tr><td>Low Pedagogy
Low Risk</td><td>Low Pedagogy
High Risk</td></tr>
</table>

PEDAGOGIC VALUE

DEGREE OF RISK

This figure is a decision square relating pedagogic value and degree of risk.

Each activity can be characterized by one of the four categories indicated. The actions required for activities in each category are described below.

- ❑ **High-pedagogy, low-risk quadrant** If the activity falls into this category, then no action is necessary because this activity fits the ideal.

- ❑ **Low-pedagogy, low-risk quadrant** If the activity falls into this category, consider eliminating this activity from your lesson plans for pedagogic reasons.

- ❑ **High-pedagogy, high-risk quadrant** If the activity falls into this category, reduce the hazards of the activity or eliminate the activity from your lesson plans.

- ❑ **Low-pedagogy, high-risk quadrant** If the activity falls into this category, eliminate the activity from your lesson plans because it is too hazardous and is not a valuable learning tool.

Prioritization of hazards

The next step in evaluating hazards is to list hazards according to likelihood of occurrence and danger. Again, the following decision square and the actions necessary for hazards that fall into each category in the decision square may help you prioritize the hazards in activities.

High Likelihood **Low Danger**	**High Likelihood** **High Danger**
Low Likelihood **Low Danger**	**Low Likelihood** **High Danger**

LIKELIHOOD OF HAZARD

DEGREE OF HAZARD

This figure is a decision square relating the likelihood of a hazard and the degree of severity of a hazard.

❏ **High-likelihood, low-danger quadrant** This type of hazard is not very dangerous, so if you can decrease the likelihood that this hazard will occur in an activity, this activity (or an aspect of this activity) is relatively safe.

❏ **Low-likelihood, low-danger quadrant** This type of hazard is not very dangerous and has little likelihood of occurring. Therefore, you need to make little to no adjustments for this hazard. This quadrant is preferred to the other quadrants for all possible hazards of an activity.

❏ **High-likelihood, high-danger quadrant** This type of hazard is dangerous and has a high likelihood of occurring. Therefore, you must reduce or eliminate the danger of this type of hazard, or you must eliminate the entire activity from your lesson plans.

❏ **Low-likelihood, high-danger quadrant** This type of hazard has little likelihood of occurring; however, if it does occur during an activity, disastrous results will follow. Therefore, you must reduce or eliminate the danger of this hazard. Even though the likelihood of this hazard is low, the consequences of this hazard cannot be ignored.

Identifying the intervention (action) line

Once the hazards are prioritized, you must decide how many of the hazards you will address. To make this decision, you must first insert an "intervention line" or "action line" in your prioritized list of hazards. All hazards listed above this line should be addressed immediately. Factors that will help you decide where to insert your intervention line are the degree of danger for each hazard, the likelihood of each hazard, and the time and resources you have available. Hazards listed below the line should not be ignored. When reviewing assessments of hazards in the future, you may notice that some of these hazards acquire increased importance or that new resources are available to deal with those hazards.

3. Select appropriate controls

What specific controls can be used to address the risks of a given activity that contains hazards listed above your intervention line? Two basic types of controls are **engineering controls** and **administrative controls.**

Engineering controls rely on four types of hazard reduction:

- ❑ **Distance** Increase the space between students and the hazardous apparatus or equipment (or between the teacher and the hazard).

- ❑ **Duration** Decrease the amount of time that students are exposed to hazardous apparatus or equipment.

- ❑ **Shielding** Place appropriate physical barriers between the hazardous apparatus or equipment and students (or teacher).

- ❑ **Substitution** Find less hazardous alternatives to apparatus or equipment.

Administrative controls can take a variety of forms. Possible administrative controls are listed below.

- ❑ Change the procedures of activities.

- ❑ Include warnings in students' handouts about the hazards that exist for each activity.

- ❑ Post signs and labels in your classroom.

- ❑ Give safety quizzes to the students. (These quizzes should be part of the students' grades, or the students will not take the quizzes seriously).

- ❑ Develop and enforce safety rules.

This list is not comprehensive—many other possibilities exist.

 SAFETY SUGGESTIONS

"Why can't I do the activity I like?"
An honest approach to risk assessment does not necessarily rule out a specific activity. Whether you can address enough of the hazards on the prioritized list determines whether you can perform an activity. Just because you don't have the resources you need to implement the activity this year does not mean you cannot plan for the activity next year.

 **DEFINITIONS**

engineering controls
interventions that reduce the risk inherent in apparatus or equipment

administrative controls
procedural steps that reduce risk in an activity

 SAFETY SUGGESTIONS

When making physical changes to an activity, be careful that an equally (or more) insidious hazard is not introduced.

4. Implement and apply the selected controls

After you have selected the appropriate controls, ensure that they are implemented. If colleagues who were not involved in the assessment process will be teaching the course, make sure they utilize the controls also. Controls that require changes in teaching methodology may be especially difficult to implement if the current methodology is well entrenched in your department. The hazards and their associated controls may need to be explicitly demonstrated to your colleagues to make clear the dangers of not implementing the necessary controls.

5. Review activities periodically, and make needed adjustments

Make periodic reviews of the activities in your curriculum. Any controls that have become ineffective should be changed or replaced with effective controls. Reexamine items on the prioritized list of hazards (see step 2), and address hazards below the intervention line. Ideally, hazards on your list should be addressed as soon as possible, but time or other resources may not always be immediately available. Therefore, a periodic review of each activity is essential, because time and other resources may become available. Note, however, that if a change causes an activity or hazard to fall into a less desirable quadrant of either of the decision squares, you must immediately change the activity to make it safer.

An application of the basic hazard assessment method

The "Specific Heats of Metals" experiment is performed in chemistry and physics classes (and perhaps in physical science classes as well), so the experiment is familiar to many. In the experiment, students heat metal samples to nearly 100°C and then place each sample in a cold-water bath. Students can then calculate the specific heat of the metal sample after determining the water's temperature change. A diagram of a typical setup for this experiment is given in the following diagram. The hazard assessment method is applied to this setup seen in the figure to show you how this method works. In addition, the assessment addresses variations of the experiment such as different heat sources and boilers.

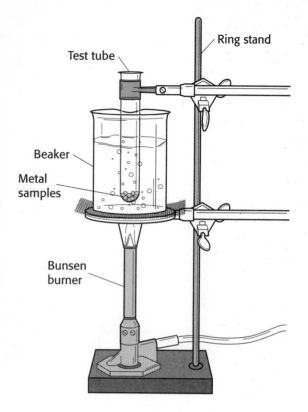

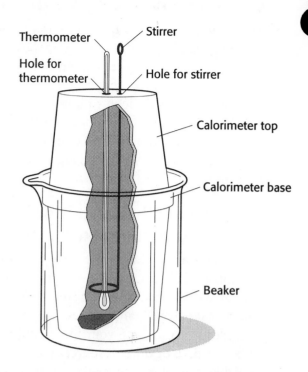

Typical apparatus used in this activity include a boiler (such as large glass beaker), a heat source (Bunsen burner or hot plate), a stand or tripod for the boiler, a calorimeter, thermometers, samples (typically samples of copper, aluminum, zinc, tin, or lead), tongs (or forceps or string) to handle samples, and a balance.

1. Identify the hazards

Below is a sample list of hazards for this experiment. Remember to remain as open-minded as possible in identifying the hazards of an activity or experiment—list all the potential hazards no matter how remote or silly they may seem.

✔ **Heat Sources (Electricity)**

  ✔ The ground prongs could be removed from the power cords.

  ✔ The power cords could be near standing water; water could also splash or leak onto the power cords.

  ✔ If too many laboratory stations exist, the circuits in the classroom could overload.

  ✔ The classroom may not have enough outlets for the number of groups planned.

  ✔ When the power cords are plugged in, they may obstruct walkways.

  ✔ The location of outlets may be near water or on table skirts that students could lean against.

CHAPTER 2

✔ **Gas/Bunsen Burners**

  ✔ The gas valves may leak, or they may be left on.

  ✔ A Bunsen burner may be dangerously lighted because of improper gas flow from a gas valve or reckless use of matches or a spark lighter.

  ✔ The open flames of Bunsen burners will ignite many materials that could come in contact with the flames.

  ✔ A Bunsen burner may have a clogged orifice.

  ✔ A Bunsen burner may have a worn O-ring on its regulator stem.

  ✔ The wrong type of burner may be used.

  ✔ Someone may use the regulating valve of a Bunsen burner as a shut-off valve (the gas valve).

  ✔ A worn or cracked tube may be used to connect a Bunsen burner to a gas valve.

  ✔ The tubing that is used to connect a Bunsen burner to a gas valve may get tangled or kinked.

  ✔ Bunsen burners may not allow for proper flame adjustment.

  ✔ Blow-back may occur during the experiment.

✔ **Calorimeters**

  ✔ A calorimeter may tip over and spill hot water and the hot sample.

  ✔ A calorimeter may leak or spill.

✔ **Safety Equipment**

  ✔ Some people may not wear their aprons (or laboratory coats) and goggles unless told repeatedly to do so.

  ✔ Gloves used in the classroom may not be suitable for heat protection.

✔ **Boilers**

  ✔ Someone may touch a hot, metal container or a glass beaker.

  ✔ A boiler may leak hot water.

  ✔ A cup that holds metal samples may tip over while samples are being removed.

  ✔ Boiling water may splash out of a boiler if too much water is put into the boiler.

  ✔ Someone may be burned by steam emitting from the boiler.

✔ If a boiler is stoppered, someone may be hurt by pressure buildup.

✔ A boiler may break.

✔ Someone may reach into the boiling water in a boiler to remove a sample.

✔ The contents of a boiler may spill if the boiler handle is in the way of a person or equipment and is hit.

✔ **Boiler Tripods**

✔ Tripod legs may not be sturdy or even.

✔ If a boiler stand is a ring stand, then the stand's rings may be missing or uneven.

✔ **Thermometers**

✔ If a thermometer is broken, mercury may spill and vaporize.

✔ A thermometer may break while someone is trying to insert the thermometer into a rubber stopper.

✔ A very long thermometer may make a calorimeter or a boiler unsteady.

✔ A thermometer may be at eye level after it is secured in a calorimeter or a boiler.

✔ **Samples**

✔ Loose eyehooks that are screwed into samples may cause injury if someone tries to pick up one of these samples by these eyehooks.

✔ Sample materials may be hazardous (lead is an example).

✔ Samples may be too large for boilers or calorimeters.

✔ Samples may break glass beakers if the samples are thrown into the beakers.

✔ **Forceps/Tongs/String**

✔ Forceps and tongs, if misused, may pinch skin.

✔ Forceps and tongs will be hot if they are left in boiling water, and the hot forceps and tongs could result in a burn.

✔ Strings that are too short may fall into sample containers or may lie against the hot sides of boilers, and strings that are too long may get tangled and pull over containers.

Note that the presence of a disability will, of necessity, extend this list. The number and variety of additional potential hazards will depend on the nature of the disability.

2. Evaluate the hazards

Below is a prioritized list of the experiment's hazards from high danger/high likelihood to low danger/low likelihood. Note that the assigned priorities will vary from teacher to teacher. Teams may even need to negotiate the placement of some items on the list. In addition, previous experiences will influence how a teacher rates a hazard.

1. The ground prongs could be removed from power cords.

2. The power cords could be near standing water; water could also splash or leak onto the power cords.

3. If too many laboratory stations exist, the circuits in the classroom could overload.

4. The classroom may not have enough outlets for the number of groups planned.

5. When the power cords are plugged in, they may obstruct walkways.

6. The location of outlets may be near water or on table skirts that students could lean against.

7. The gas valves may leak, or they may be left on.

8. A Bunsen burner may be dangerously lighted because of improper gas flow from a gas valve or reckless use of matches or a spark lighter.

9. The open flames of Bunsen burners will ignite many materials that could come in contact with the flames.

10. A Bunsen burner may have a clogged orifice.

11. A Bunsen burner may have a worn O-ring on its regulator stem.

12. The wrong type of burner may be used.

13. Someone may use the regulating valve of a Bunsen burner as a shut-off valve (the gas valve).

14. A worn or cracked tube may be used to connect a Bunsen burner to a gas valve.

15. The tubing that is used to connect a Bunsen burner to a gas valve may get tangled or kinked.

16. Bunsen burners may not allow for proper flame adjustment.

17. Blow-back may occur during the experiment.

18. Someone may touch a hot, metal container or a glass beaker.

19. A boiler may leak hot water.

20. A cup that holds metal samples may tip over while samples are being removed.

21. Boiling water may splash out of a boiler if too much water is put into the boiler.

22. Someone may be burned by steam emitting from the boiler.

23. If a boiler is stoppered, someone may be hurt by pressure buildup.

24. A boiler may break.

25. Someone may reach into the boiling water in a boiler to remove a sample.

26. The contents of a boiler may spill if the boiler handle is in the way of a person or equipment and is hit.

27. Some people may not wear their aprons (or laboratory coats) and goggles unless told repeatedly to do so.

28. Gloves used in the classroom may not be suitable for heat protection.

29. Tripod legs may not be sturdy or even.

30. If a boiler stand is a ring stand, then the stand's rings may be missing or uneven.

31. A calorimeter may tip over and spill hot water and the hot sample.

32. A calorimeter may leak or spill.

33. If a thermometer is broken, mercury may spill and vaporize.

34. A thermometer may break while someone is trying to insert the thermometer into a rubber stopper.

35. A very long thermometer may make a calorimeter or a boiler unsteady.

36. A thermometer may be at eye level after it is secured in a calorimeter or a boiler.

37. Loose eyehooks that are screwed into samples may cause injury if someone tries to pick up one of these samples by these eyehooks.

38. Sample materials may be hazardous (lead is an example).

39. Samples may be too large for boilers or calorimeters.

40. Samples may break glass beakers if the samples are thrown into the beakers.

41. Forceps and tongs, if misused, may pinch skin.

42. Forceps and tongs will be hot if they are left in boiling water, and the hot forceps and tongs could result in a burn.

43. Strings that are too short may fall into sample containers or may lie against the hot sides of boilers, and strings that are too long may get tangled and pull over containers.

Based on degree and likelihood of each hazard and the factor of time, the intervention line is placed between hazard 28 and hazard 29. How should some of the 43 hazards be addressed?

3. Select controls

In this example, financial considerations play a lesser role in selecting controls than other considerations, such as time, play. Most of the controls listed here are low tech and low cost and can be easily addressed by a teacher.

✔ **Heating Sources**

✔ Decide which heating source is most appropriate given the setup of the classroom.

✔ If gas burners must be used, then inspect them when you set up the laboratory stations. Your gas burners should be of the correct type for the gas and gas valves in your classroom. A quick visual check of the burners between classes ensures that no damaged burners will be used. Always check that gas outlets are completely turned off after the burners are no longer needed during a class.

✔ An electric boiler in which the plug is attached to the boiler base should not be used because of the electrical hazard of having a power cord so near water.

✔ Overall, however, an electrical heating source seems less hazardous than a gas heating source seems. A commercial hot plate is relatively inexpensive, and two stations can share one hot plate. However, hot plates do have exposed heating coils, and people must be careful not to splash water onto the plug or outlet. Warning labels and signs about the coils could be placed on the sides of hot plates (if the hot plates do not become too hot), on the tables or walls near the laboratory stations, or in handouts. A more expensive but somewhat safer alternative to hot plates would be hot plates with ceramic tops.

✔ Electric outlets can be a major concern if there are not enough of them or if they are in inconvenient locations. Unfortunately, there is little you can do about this situation, short of a major renovation of your classroom. The best location for this activity is on tables against walls. If outlets are located on the table skirt, you must ensure

CHAPTER 2

that students leaning against the table do not lean against the plugs or cords. Repeatedly leaning against the plugs may loosen them from the outlets, expose the prongs on the plug, and create an electric shock hazard. (This is why it is better to have outlets installed with the ground prong on top—if the ground prong becomes exposed, the possibility of an electric shock hazard is lessened.)

✔ Extension cords should not be used. If there are insufficient outlets to accommodate the number of laboratory stations, then students should do the activity in shifts. Increasing the number of students at a station is also not advisable because having students work in close quarters will create more congestion and increase the risk of accidents.

✔ Boilers

✔ The safest boiler to use is the standard model available in most catalogs of scientific apparatus. These boilers will not break if they are accidentally tipped over, and they will not spill their contents quite as quickly or over as random an area as a glass beaker or household pot will. (The water level indicator tubes on these boilers could break, however.)

✔ Although household pots or pans may be the cheapest and most readily available "boilers," their handles can get in the path of people and equipment, especially in crowded facilities. Water is also more likely to be splashed if these pots and pans are used. Someone putting his or her hand in the pot is also a remote possibility.

✔ Thermometers

✔ Try to find thermometers that do not contain mercury. Thermometers breaking (and perhaps stabbing hands) while students insert the thermometers into rubber stoppers are a common laboratory accident. This rubber-stopper hazard can be addressed by substituting the stopper with a folded paper towel that has a hole in it. Place the paper towel on the sample cup, and insert the thermometer through the hole. This method may not be as efficient as the stopper, but it is safer to use.

✔ Thermometers can be physical hazards if the thermometers are very long—they can make calorimeters or boilers unstable and are often at eye level during the course of the experiment. Calorimeters or boilers may be prevented from becoming unstable by using thermometer clamps attached to ring stands to hold the thermometers in an upright position. If funds are available, the best alternative is to use a multimeter with a temperature unit

CHAPTER 2

and probe. If only one multimeter for each station is practical, the multimeter should be used in the hot sample cup.

✔ **Samples**

  ✔ Be aware that screws tend to loosen in metal materials and that the holes drilled in metal samples often do not remain tapped. Strings should not be so long that they dangle into the heat sources or become tangled in the apparatus. Strings should not be so short that they are hazardous to grasp because they are lying against the hot sides of the boilers. Students could be told to use a pen or pencil to pull the string away from the boiler before grasping the string.

  ✔ Tongs probably will not fit inside the hot sample cup easily enough to be practical or safe. Forceps or larger tweezers may not hold a sample securely enough for the time necessary to complete the transfer.

  ✔ The samples should be of materials that will not create controversy.

  ✔ The samples should be not be too large or too irregularly shaped to fit easily into the containers and to be easily transferred from one container to the other. Solid samples of reasonable size are preferable to shot or powder samples because these small particles are easy to spill.

✔ **Safety Equipment**

  ✔ Supply each student with goggles and a laboratory apron (or coat) in case of splashes or spills of boiling water.

  ✔ Gloves for heat protection while transferring the samples are probably more of a hindrance in this case, because some degree of dexterity is necessary for this experiment. You will need to warn students not to touch the hot sides of the boiler or other components that may get very warm because of conduction.

  ✔ As a general rule, students should not wear loose jewelry or loose clothing in the classroom. These loose items may get caught or tangled in apparatus and lead to accidents.

✔ **Other Issues**

  ✔ Several hazards can be addressed when setting up the classroom for this experiment. Try to locate laboratory stations away from sinks and away from the edges of tables. The preferable location for laboratory stations is against a wall. This arrangement eliminates the chance of students accidentally bumping into apparatus behind them. Try to arrange power cords such that they do not create trip hazards or become entangled in other apparatus. Plenty of paper towels should be available to clean up spills. A mop and bucket for large spills are appropriate.

Many of the hazards listed on p. 14 can be controlled by posting signs in the classroom at the appropriate locations and by including warnings in the instructional materials for the activity. Of course, instructing the students about the various hazards that they will encounter is also important. A safety quiz may be appropriate before doing this experiment.

This discussion focused on general categories to prevent the discussion from becoming excessively long. In a specific assessment, hazards should be considered separately and extensively. Site-specific assessments, however, will have fewer equipment options, so the list will not be as long. Occasionally, a few hazards can be treated as a group, but doing so should not become a habit because some hazards can be hidden in the groupings.

4. Implement the controls

After proper controls have been identified, implementing the controls is essential. Funds may be a problem, but this process can be helpful in establishing budget priorities. Significant hazards can be used as leverage to acquire additional funding. The information gained in a hazard assessment can help you establish a plan for future purchases or show supervisors how future curriculum should be developed.

5. Review and update

After initial implementation of controls, review the experiment for safety and pedagogic effectiveness, and make any alterations to the experiment that are needed. Make periodic reviews to ensure that the controls continue to be effective and to judge whether any modifications are needed. The frequency of this review will depend on the frequency of changes made to the experiment, the aging of the apparatus, the availability of improved apparatus or instructional technique, and changes in standards or regulations.

Parting words

The more activities you assess with this basic hazard assessment method, the more familiar with the method you will become and the easier assessing activities will become. While this hazard assessment method is relatively simple, it should provide a helpful perspective of activities and should lead to a safer implementation of these activities.

PHYSICAL HAZARDS

What are physical hazards?

Physical hazards are commonly found in the laboratory. These hazards are ubiquitous yet probably receive the least consideration because many of their consequences can be relatively minor injuries. In spite of their minor consequences, physical hazards should not be taken lightly. Although exposure to a physical hazard might initially produce minor injury to a student, an ultimate consequence may be that the student becomes uncomfortable in laboratory situations.

Physical hazards originate from

❑ the faulty construction of apparatus or fixtures

❑ the nonpowered or nonmechanical motion of an object

❑ the process of assembling, repairing, or setting up apparatus

❑ ergonomic factors

Some hazards that one may consider physical hazards have their origin in other categories of hazards and will be discussed later.

Moving objects can be dangerous

Moving objects are hazards that are typically found in physics or physical science activities, although some chemistry activities can create projectiles during a sudden release of pressure. These hazards are also not necessarily a part of a procedure, but they can occur as an extension of or upon completion of a procedure. Any time moving objects are present, whether they are balls, carts, cylinders, or hoops, provisions must be made to contain these objects.

Projectiles

Any projectile can be dangerous to students and teachers in the classroom. Metal projectiles, however, are an especially serious concern. Unfortunately, metal projectiles are often unavoidable in classrooms because projectile-range experiments and some demonstrations require steel balls to be launched across the room. Read the following accident scenario and accompanying tips to help avoiding a laboratory accident involving a projectile.

 ### ACCIDENT SCENARIO

Projectiles

In a crowded high school physics classroom, students are projecting balls by using catapults that the students constructed and are measuring where the balls land in relation to the catapults. A student calls to her partner who is taking a range measurement, just as a neighboring station launches its projectile. Her partner stands up and moves so that she can have a better view of the student.

Unfortunately, the partner is then hit by the neighboring station's projectile.

Tips to avoid projectile accidents

✔ Provide impact-resistant goggles to all students.

✔ Provide catch boxes to minimize the degree to which projectiles bounce or roll throughout the room.

✔ Use a softer projectile, especially if there is insufficient or crowded space.

✔ Lay out firing paths that do not overlap.

✔ Do not allow students to lean into or walk across projectile paths.

✔ Have students announce when they are going to fire so that others can move out of the way.

✔ If you have a crowded classroom, consider having only two groups of students or reconfiguring the experiment into a teacher demonstration.

Objects that are attached to apparatus may become projectiles if they separate from the apparatus. Examples include anything that has a hanging mass and may be spun, such as a hand-driven centripetal force apparatus or spinning disks on which objects are placed. Here are some tips that may help you avoid an accident involving an object that becomes a projectile during an experiment:

✔ Have students wear impact-resistant goggles.

✔ Always check objects that enclose some part of the apparatus (for example, a glass or metal tube through which a string passes). Always check the integrity of strings for fraying and the tubes through which string passes for burrs or sharp edges.

✔ Be sure all parts are firmly attached; tighten knots, screws, or fittings.

✔ When possible, wrap enclosing sleeves or tubes so that in the event of breakage pieces are contained.

✔ Do not use excessive rotating speeds; use only the lowest speeds that will provide good results.

✔ Use the lightest spinning objects possible.

 **SAFE LABS**

Experiments involving projectiles are often dangerous, especially in crowded classrooms. To minimize the danger, perform projectile labs as teacher demonstrations. To keep students involved during the demonstrations, have students

✔ construct projectiles or apparatus

✔ help you with the experiment

✔ guess which projectile will travel the farthest

✔ guess which apparatus will cause a projectile to travel the farthest

✔ Keep the work area free of obstructions. Make sure that nothing can interfere with the motion of the device and that obstructions are at least several inches beyond the maximum radius of the motion.

Falling objects

Falling objects are found in a variety of settings. They may not even be an intended part of the activity. Examples of objects that can be dangerous if they fall from a laboratory bench are clamped glassware such as thermometers, objects on balances, free-fall or Atwood machines, dropped magnets, or picket fences for free-fall motion studies. These tips should help you avoid accidents caused by falling objects in the classroom:

✔ Have students wear impact-resistant safety goggles.

✔ Always provide catch boxes to contain the falling objects. Provide padding in the catch boxes so that the objects will not bounce out or break on impact.

✔ Check clamps before each activity so that they are not too loose or too tight.

✔ Make sure students know how to use the types of clamps they encounter.

✔ Use balances that have pans instead of plates, or instruct students on how to place the object on the plate so that it will not roll off (for example, place carts upside down on a plate).

Bouncing/rolling objects

Some activities require students to roll balls or cans down ramps or push carts across the floor. Bouncing or rolling objects can be just as dangerous as falling objects or projectiles. Read the following scenario and tips to minimize the risk of student injury from bouncing or rolling objects.

 ## ACCIDENT SCENARIO ——————————————

Rolling Objects

In a high school physical science classroom, students are determining the amount of time that balls of various sizes take to roll down an inclined plane. One student is supposed to catch each of the balls after it leaves the inclined plane at his laboratory station. The student fails to catch a ball, and it rolls onto the floor. The ball then rolls down an aisle, and a student at another station steps back onto the ball. As a result, the student loses his balance, falls, and strikes his head on the edge of a laboratory table. What began as a rather innocuous laboratory activity ends as a potentially serious accident.

Tips to avoid an accident involving a rolling object

✔ Have students wear impact-resistant safety goggles.

✔ Do not set up apparatus so that an object may accidentally roll out of the classroom.

✔ Design activities so that hallways are not needed for an activity.

✔ Provide barriers, curbs, or catch boxes to prevent objects from uncontrolled bouncing or rolling.

✔ Arrange curbs or barriers at the end of the run or around the edge of the table to contain objects.

✔ If tracks are being used, make sure the end stops or barriers provided are securely in place.

✔ Always keep the path of motion free of obstructions.

✔ Warn neighboring students when an activity is about to start.

✔ Develop procedural controls that minimize these hazards. For example,

✔ do not allow students to roll objects faster than necessary to obtain good data

✔ at the end of the activity, have students place the objects where they cannot become hazards (have students turn carts upside down, return objects to you, or place potentially hazardous objects in boxes so that the objects will not roll).

Some objects have inherent dangers

Physical hazards may be created just by the way apparatus must be set up or by the way a tool is used. An object mounted at eye level can be hazardous if someone walks into it. Students walking by may accidentally snag skin and clothing on protruding objects. Equipment set up in an awkward position may cause discomfort to the user of the equipment, especially over a long period of time. Pinch (or nip) points can be found on many types of pliers or tweezers. Listed below are general tips to deal with these hazards.

✔ Do not leave clamp parts protruding into walkways unless absolutely necessary; place clamps as far into the edge of the table as possible (to minimize the amount of protrusion of each clamp). Make sure that the torque rods of clamps are pushed toward the table and not in the area of traffic.

✔ Do not mount clamps or other apparatus at eye level, even if goggles are available.

✔ Do not place rods, tracks, or rails such that they protrude into walkways.

✔ Warn students not to pinch or catch body parts when the students are using tools or equipment.

✔ Set up apparatus so that students do not have to strain or maintain awkward positions for any length of time.

✔ When setting up equipment, take into account that not all students are the same height and that some students have visual or mobility impairments.

Physical hazards can also be inherent in the furniture and fixtures of a classroom. Use the following suggestions to avoid student accidents:

✔ Make sure furniture edges and corners are rounded.

✔ Encase metal edges in foam or other suitable soft padding.

✔ Do not place furniture or store objects where they may create a trip hazard.

✔ Make sure paths to exits are clear.

✔ Have custodial staff use nonslip wax, especially if water spills are common.

✔ Have damaged furniture and fixtures repaired or replaced as soon as possible.

✔ Do not allow students to lay coats, bags, or any other items where they can catch on gas outlet valves or electrical plugs.

✔ Do not use furniture or fixtures for anything but their intended purpose, even if the planned alternate use is momentary.

✔ When arranging furniture, take into account that not all students are the same height or that some students have visual or mobility impairments.

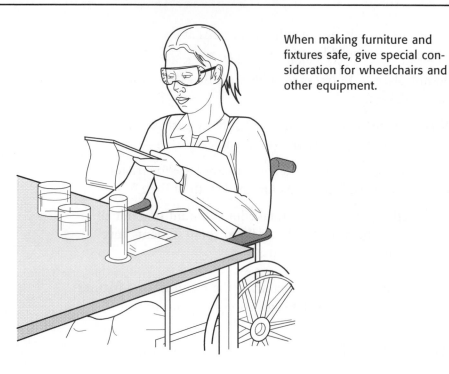

When making furniture and fixtures safe, give special consideration for wheelchairs and other equipment.

Sharp or pointed objects

Sharp or pointed objects are a special safety concern in the classroom, but they are almost unavoidable during many experiments. Certain projects require students to shape materials by cutting or punching. Cone bearings, geology field tools (rock picks, chisels, and soil samplers), and screwdrivers have sharp or pointed ends, as do many clamps. Certain attachments to apparatus may contain sharp edges or corners. Cheaper apparatus may have rough or unfinished surfaces, giving rise to metal whiskers or splinters. Some safety tips are listed below.

✔ Ensure that projects are commensurate with the age and sophistication of the students.

✔ Ensure that students receive instruction in the safest and most efficient means of performing necessary activities involving cutting or punching.

✔ Use the safest types of tools that are designed to perform the required work (for example, use utility knives instead of razor blades and round-nose scissors instead of pointed scissors).

✔ Whenever possible, mount pointed clamps above head height.

✔ Encase or cover sharp or pointed ends. Plastic dips, adhesive-backed felt, or tape are options for encasing material.

✔ Sand or file rough surfaces and whiskers.

✔ Fill in uneven surfaces with plastic, wood, putty, or any other proper material.

✔ Remove or repair splintered surfaces.

Heavy objects

Heavy masses are occasionally needed to hold objects down during a laboratory experiment. In addition, some experimental apparatus are heavy and unstable. Any of these unsecured objects situated near the edge of a table may accidentally be pulled over the edge and cause an injury. To avoid injury by a heavy, unsecured object in the classroom, follow the tips in the list below.

✔ Do not mount heavy objects close to the table edge; otherwise, try to clamp them to the table edge.

✔ Do not use free-standing bases and rods to help support heavy equipment if mounting holes are provided in the tabletop.

✔ Take care to keep the center of mass of objects as low as possible (do not set up apparatus such that the apparatus are unstable).

✔ Keep clear the areas in which heavy apparatus might fall.

✔ Do not let students sit with their legs or feet under heavy equipment.

✔ Do not allow students to play with heavy masses.

CHAPTER 3

MECHANICAL HAZARDS

What are mechanical hazards?

Mechanical hazards are created by the powered operation of apparatus or tools. The applied power may be electrical or human. Tools or apparatus have three locations where mechanical hazards can exist:

- ❏ the point of operation
- ❏ the point of power transmission
- ❏ the area of moving parts

The point of operation is where the action is taking place—a drill bit, the sandpaper on a palm sander, or the vibrating tine on a string vibrator. The point of power transmission is where the applied energy is converted to work; two examples of the point of power transmission are the pulleys and belt on a centripetal force apparatus and the axle on a motor-driven rotator. The area of moving parts involves any actions between the point of operation and the point of power transmission. Examples of moving parts are the gears or pulleys on an apparatus, the sharp or protruding points or hardware on pulleys, and shafts or arms.

Apparatus or tools that rotate

Rotating apparatus or tools can be dangerous because they can catch and twist a student's clothing, hair, or jewelry and can cause serious damage to the student. Even slowly rotating objects can snag something on a student and force an arm or hand into a precarious position. A few examples of rotation hazards are

- ❏ drill bits
- ❏ gears in Wimshurst machines
- ❏ centrifuge rotors
- ❏ governors for demonstrating centrifugal force
- ❏ electric motor shafts
- ❏ rotators for spinning discs, wheels, centrifugal forces rotors, or other equipment
- ❏ projections (nuts, set screws, nicks, and abrasions) from rotating parts

 DID YOU KNOW? ——————————————

Hand centrifuges

Hand centrifuges are serious potential hazards. Cranked by hand and clamped to the edge of a table, hand centrifuges spin two glass centrifuge tubes at speeds of up to 2,000 rpm. As purchased, the tubes are not shielded in any way. If a neighboring student is not careful, he or she could turn into or back into the whirling tubes. The tubes may not break completely as a result of a student backing into them, and the jagged edges of the newly broken glass tubes can injure the student. Regardless of whether the tubes break completely, a good possibility exists for broken glass to fly about the classroom and injure students.

Precautions for working with hand and power tools

Some projects, such as those for science fairs, require a degree of advanced object-shaping, which is accomplished by using tools or apparatus that can cut, punch, shear, or bend sturdy materials. Tools and apparatus that can manipulate or cut sturdy material can, of course, also seriously injure a student. Hazards are usually found at the point of operation on such devices. An associated hazard that may arise is flying chips or shavings from the material while it is being cut. Emphasize to students that work with these types of tools should be done only under direct adult supervision. In addition, make sure the students are capable of safely using the necessary tools. Listed below are some safety tips and precautions to bear in mind when using various hand and power tools.

✔ **General**

  ✔ Make sure the project area is well lighted and uncluttered.

  ✔ Visually inspect tools, power cords, and accessories before allowing students to use them.

  ✔ Ensure that machine and work area guards and shields are in place and are being used.

  ✔ Include appropriate warning notices at the project area and in instructional materials.

  ✔ Ensure that projects are commensurate with the age and sophistication of the students.

  ✔ Demonstrate the safe use of tools, and discuss any concerns that students may have about operating equipment.

  ✔ Always have students wear impact-resistant goggles.

  ✔ Do not permit students to wear loose clothing or jewelry when using power tools. Make students tie back long hair.

  ✔ Limit the use of gloves when using hand tools—gloves can be too bulky for a good grip, and they limit the "feel" for the tool.

  ✔ Make sure that students focus on the task at hand; eliminate distractions.

✔ Enforce the rule of using the proper tool for the task.

✔ Never leave a running tool unattended. In addition, tell students that they may never leave a running tool unattended.

✔ Keep the project area clean and free of scraps.

✔ **Knives**

✔ Do not allow students to use dull or notched blades.

✔ Never allow students to test a cutting edge with their fingers (students should use scrap material for testing a cutting edge).

✔ Remind students to keep their hands and body clear of the knife stroke; make sure that neighboring students are also clear of the work area.

✔ Make sure that students always cut away from their bodies.

✔ **Hammers**

✔ Check the condition of a hammer before allowing students to use it. Do not use hammers that have loose heads or cracked handles.

✔ Provide the proper hammer for the project—if too light, a hammer bounces in the user's hand; if too heavy, a hammer is hard to control.

✔ Make sure that students have an unobstructed area to use the hammer.

✔ Remind students to keep their fingers away from the object being hammered.

✔ **Screwdrivers**

✔ Remind students that screwdrivers are not to be hammered or used as chisels, punches, awls, or levers.

✔ Do not let students hold an object in one hand and use a screwdriver with the other hand; place the object on a bench or table or in a vise.

✔ Do not use noninsulated screwdrivers in electrical projects.

✔ **Wrenches**

✔ To minimize sudden slips, remind students to stand in a balanced position and to avoid reaching for awkward or distant locations while using a wrench.

✔ Tell students to always pull on the wrench handle instead of pushing against the fixed jaw.

✔ Use the proper size wrench for the nut or bolt.

✔ If students are using adjustable wrenches, make sure that they keep the open jaws facing toward them to reduce slippage.

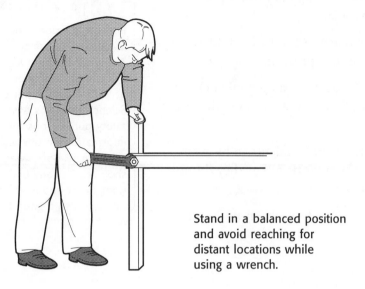

Stand in a balanced position and avoid reaching for distant locations while using a wrench.

✔ Pliers

✔ Remind students that pliers are not to be used in place of hammers or wrenches.

✔ Do not use noninsulated pliers in electrical projects.

✔ Files

✔ Never allow a student to use a file without a handle—the tang can pierce the student's palm or wrist if the file slips or catches.

✔ Power hand tools

✔ Make sure that the students are old enough and mature enough to use the tool.

✔ Always inspect power tools before allowing students to use them.

✔ Make certain that students receive proper training in the use of the tool.

✔ Do not permit students to carry power tools by the electrical cord.

✔ Ensure that guards are used on all tools that have such devices.

✔ Make sure that students do not try to use a power tool before it has reached operating speed or while it is coming to a stop.

✔ Never let students try to stop a tool's moving parts by hand or with other objects—let the tool coast to a stop by itself.

✔ Tell students to never lay a tool down before it has come to a complete stop.

✔ Do not allow students to force a power tool into the material.

✔ Be sure the material can be held safely in place during the operation.

✔ Do not let students stand directly behind or in front of a tool that is in use, in case it malfunctions.

✔ Continually remind students to be aware of a tool's power cord so that they do not accidentally cut it.

✔ Disconnect power tools when not in use.

 SAFETY INFORMATION

Interested readers may refer to the Occupational Safety and Health Administration's (OSHA's) Code of Federal Regulations, Title 29, part 1910 and to various National Science Teacher's Association (NSTA) safety publications for more detailed information on physical and mechanical hazards. Borrowing from a local shop teacher any books or publications he or she might have on tool safety is also a good idea.

CHEMICAL HAZARDS

What are chemical hazards?

A chemical hazard is a chemical whose properties jeopardize the health of humans and other animals or whose properties harm the environment. A chemical hazard is also a chemical that, when used improperly, can produce a physical or health risk.

How are hazardous chemicals categorized?

Chemicals must come in contact with living tissue or the environment to cause harm. Inhalation, ingestion, injection, and direct contact with skin or eyes are ways that chemicals can come into contact with living tissue. Hazardous chemicals can come in contact with the environment by being spilled, poured down drains, or stored improperly. (For example, improper storage can allow volatile chemicals into the atmosphere.) To inform teachers, experimenters, and other users of chemical hazards, scientists have categorized chemicals in several ways. Some classification systems take into account only the health risks chemicals pose whereas other systems take into account the health and physical (environmental) risks of chemicals.

Some categories for a comprehensive classification scheme

A comprehensive classification scheme may be rather involved because many chemicals can be classified in more than one category. A few basic categories are as follows:

❏ **Reactive** Chemicals that react violently with water to produce toxic gases or explosive mixtures are classified as reactive.

  examples: sodium, potassium, and lithium

❏ **Irritant (allergen, sensitizer)** Irritants are chemicals that cause a reversible inflammatory effect at the site of contact with living tissue. People can have different responses to irritants. Some chemicals that are considered irritants have little effect on some people but cause serious health problems for others.

  examples: hexane, carbon tetrachloride, sodium silicate, hydrogen chloride, and sodium hydroxide

❏ **Corrosive** Chemicals are corrosive if they cause the visible destruction of or irreversible alterations in living tissue.

  examples: strong acids, strong bases, dehydrating agents, and oxidizing agents

❏ **Toxic** Toxic chemicals are harmful on contact with living tissue, whether by direct contact, inhalation, injection, or ingestion. This classification can also include carcinogens,

 SAFETY SUGGESTIONS

The safe use of chemicals during an experiment requires you and your students to be respectful of and aware of the dangers of chemicals. Therefore, you should learn the basic skills needed for safe chemical usage, storage, and disposal and learn the applicable federal, state, and local regulations. You should then teach your students how to handle chemicals safely.

CHAPTER 5

mutagens, and teratogens all of which should not be in classroom laboratories.

examples: methyl alcohol, sodium sulfate, lead, hydrogen chloride, and sodium hydroxide

❏ **Flammable** Chemicals that catch fire and burn in air are classified as flammable. (Flammable liquids do not burn but their vapors do.)

examples: acetone and alcohols

❏ **Oxidizer** Oxidizers are chemicals that readily yield oxygen to enhance combustion of other materials.

examples: nitric acid, nitrate compounds, nitrite compounds, and permanganate compounds

What does the law require?

The law requires the safe handling of chemicals in the classroom. Read the following sections to find out who creates these laws and what some of the laws are.

Who creates the laws?

The U.S. Department of Occupational Safety and Health Administration (OSHA) creates federal regulations regarding the safe handling of chemicals (and other potential health hazards) and enforces these regulations to ensure that classrooms and other workplaces are safe. This department was created by Congress in 1971 under the Occupational Safety and Health Act and has a budget of more than $400 million. Two codes that OSHA created and that pertain to you and your classroom are the Laboratory Safety Standard and the Hazard Communication Standard. These standards are referred to throughout this chapter. Another set of standards that are referred to in this chapter are from the American National Standards Institute (ANSI), a nonprofit, private organization dedicated to standardizing conditions in workplaces. ANSI does not create standards but compiles them from other sources (such as OSHA). In addition, compliance with ANSI is voluntary; the organization does not enforce any regulations.

 DEFINITIONS

carcinogen
a chemical that is thought to have or has potential to cause cancer

mutagen
a chemical that is thought to have or has potential to cause mutations of genetic structure

teratogen
a chemical that is thought to have or has potential to cause malformations of a fetus

 **DID YOU KNOW?**

PELs and TLVs

A chemical can also be classified by the exposure needed to harm a person. One classification is called the permissible exposure level (PEL), which is the highest concentration of a chemical to which a person can be exposed during an average workday. Another classification is called the threshold limit value (TLV). There are three categories of TLVs, but all categories pertain to the concentration of a chemical to which a person can be exposed for a specified period of time (periods range from instantaneously to the length of a career). PELs have been created by the OSHA for approximately 550 chemicals, and TLVs have been created by the American Conference of Governmental Industrial Hygienists (ACGIH) for about 850 chemicals.

Create a chemical hygiene plan

OSHA's Laboratory Safety Standard mandates that workplaces that use hazardous chemicals must have a chemical hygiene plan (CHP). A chemical hygiene plan can help protect you and your students from health hazards in your classroom because the plan provides safety guidelines for anyone in the presence of the hazardous chemicals in your classroom. However, for the plan to work, it must be readily available to everyone who works in the classroom. A copy of your plan should be kept in a prominent place near the entrance to the classroom. In the event of an accident, your plan must also be available to emergency personnel.

 **DID YOU KNOW?**

The number of occupational injuries has dropped by 40 percent since OSHA was established.

Some of the sections of a chemical hygiene plan are, by nature, general enough to apply to all classrooms at a given school. However, your chemical hygiene plan must be specific enough to address the particular hazards found in your classroom. If only one or two classrooms at your school need a chemical hygiene plan, the specific procedures can be worked into the body of a shared plan. If many classrooms at your school need a chemical hygiene plan, specific procedures for each classroom may be attached as addenda to the general core of the plan.

Because teachers, students, and staff are responsible for implementing a CHP, all should participate in creating a plan. This joint effort ensures that everyone is aware of his or her responsibilities and provides a more practical plan. A chemical hygiene plan consists of several parts, each of which must be documented in writing:

❑ **General principles** This part of the CHP provides the basic principles of chemical use that everyone should strive to meet: Minimize exposure. Do not underestimate risk. Ensure adequate ventilation. Institute a chemical hygiene plan. Observe exposure limits.

❑ **Responsibilities** This part of the CHP lists who is responsible for what, from administrative levels down to the end user.

❑ **The laboratory facility** The general requirements for the design, maintenance, usage, and ventilation of laboratories (including storage and preparatory rooms) are delineated in this section of the CHP.

❑ **Basic rules and procedures** The general rules for working in the laboratory as well as rules for dealing with specific classes of chemical hazards are included in this section of the CHP.

❑ **Chemical procurement, distribution, and storage** The procedures for receiving shipments and for distributing and storing chemicals are provided in this part of the plan.

CHAPTER 5

❏ **Environmental monitoring** This section of the plan includes procedures for regular monitoring of the environment. (These procedures should not be necessary for a teaching laboratory, although they may be appropriate in storage areas. Periodic monitoring is required for hoods and is recommended for ventilation [HVAC] equipment. Laboratory monitoring may be necessary for certain activities to ensure that exposure limits are being observed.)

❏ **Housekeeping, maintenance, and inspections** A statement that establishes who is responsible for cleaning and maintaining the laboratory and its equipment is made in this section of the CHP. (This section also establishes schedules for inspecting the safety equipment and the cleanliness of a laboratory. Regular lab apparatus [for example, centrifuges, and burners] should be included in the inspection and maintenance program.)

❏ **Medical program** Statements that address how first aid cases will be handled are made in this section of the plan. (Ongoing medical monitoring should be limited to those teachers, if any, who handle the most hazardous chemicals on a regular basis.)

❏ **Personal protective apparel and equipment** A list of the apparel and equipment necessary for each laboratory is provided in this part of the plan.

❏ **Records** Forms for recording and maintaining accident reports, exposure-related medical consultations or exams, the chemical hygiene plan, chemical inventory, and medical records are provided in this part of the CHP.

❏ **Signs and labels** General signs and labels listing emergency contact numbers, locations of safety equipment, warnings of specific hazards, and waste containers are included in this part of the CHP.

❏ **Spills and accidents** The procedures for spill control, loss of ventilation, accidents, evacuation, and drills are delineated in this section of the CHP.

❏ **Information and training program** Information that ensures that anyone at risk from a classroom hazard receives information and training on a regular basis to help him or her safely deal with those risks is provided in this part of the plan.

❏ **Waste disposal program** Guidelines for how chemical wastes will be handled are delineated in this section of the CHP.

❑ **Safety recommendations** This part of the CHP includes recommendations for handling associated hazards that might be found in the classroom. (Examples of hazards include compressed gas/cryogenic cylinders, electrical equipment, and pressurized apparatus.)

❑ **Material safety data sheets (MSDS)** An MSDS for each chemical used in a classroom is provided in this section of the plan. (In addition, master files of MSDSs should be kept with a copy of your CHP in the school's main office and in the school district's administration building.)

Attend training programs, and ensure that students know about hazardous chemicals in the classroom

Exposure to hazardous chemicals can be greatly reduced by implementing a hazard awareness and training program. In addition, OSHA's Hazard Communication Standard specifically requires training in

❑ the detection of chemical releases by noting visual clues and odor

❑ the hazards of chemicals used and of associated equipment

❑ the methods of personal protection, including the use of personal protective equipment, experiment procedures, and techniques and emergency procedures

❑ the details of a chemical hygiene plan

If your school has no access to a training program, inform your administration that the law requires you to have training in handling hazardous chemicals. All individuals who may be exposed to hazardous chemicals should be informed of the hazards of each chemical so that they can safely use the chemicals. So, the following information should be provided to you, other faculty, staff, and students:

❑ contents of the Laboratory Safety Standard

❑ contents of your chemical hygiene plan

❑ proper handling procedures for chemicals

❑ recommended exposure limits for chemicals and the signs and symptoms of exposure to these chemicals

❑ location of reference materials, including material safety data sheets

❑ proper procedures for cleaning certain chemical spills

 SAFETY SUGGESTIONS

A teacher should often test students on their understanding of safety precautions and chemical hazards. Testing students at the beginning of the school year is not enough.

What can one teacher do given the dangers and laws regarding chemicals?

The regulations regarding chemical hazards can be intimidating. Do not give up! You can do many things to make your classroom safe during experiments. Some tips are listed in the following sections.

Learn about the chemicals in your storeroom

A material safety data sheet (MSDS) provides information about a chemical. OSHA mandates that an MSDS accompany the receipt of an order of a chemical. You have the right to send any chemical back that does not come with an MSDS. According to OSHA's Laboratory Safety Standard, copies of the MSDSs for the classroom must also be available to anyone in the classroom and to emergency personnel.

Because every chemical should come with an MSDS, some people will erroneously conclude that all chemicals are too hazardous to use. But the idea that all chemicals are too hazardous to use is somewhat exaggerated. Just treat all chemicals with caution even if you do not feel they are particularly hazardous.

A standard format for an MSDS does not exist, so the MSDSs from one supplier may look different from those of another supplier. The OSHA-recommended format is as follows:

- ❏ **Identity** The identity listed in an MSDS should match the identity on the chemical's label. This identity should be the IUPAC name but may include common names or synonyms.

- ❏ **Physical and chemical characteristics** The properties of the chemical, such as vapor pressure, density, and flash point, are usually listed.

- ❏ **Physical hazards** This category includes the reactivity of the chemical and the chemical's potential for fire and explosion.

- ❏ **Health hazards** The MSDS lists not only are the health hazards of the chemical but also the signs and symptoms (and recognized medical conditions) of exposure to the chemical.

- ❏ **Primary routes of entry** This category lists the chemical's primary routes of entry, such as ingestion or injection, into living tissue.

- ❏ **Exposure limit values** This category includes the PEL and the TLV, if established, for the chemical.

- ❏ **Carcinogenic information** Any information such as the target organs that the chemical affects is listed under this category.

❑ **Safe handling and use** Any applicable precautions when using the chemical, including hygiene and spill/leak cleanup procedures, are listed under this category.

❑ **Control measures** Some control measures for the chemical include appropriate personal protective equipment, work practices, and control procedures.

❑ **Emergency and first-aid procedures** These procedures are to be used when living tissue or the environment comes in contact with the chemical.

❑ **Date of preparation or most recent update** This date indicates when the chemical was produced or when the chemical was altered.

❑ **Contact information for the supplier of the chemical** The address and phone number of the chemical supplier is listed under this category.

Understand chemical labels, and use them

Labels are useful because they can quickly reveal the hazards of chemicals or equipment. For example, the colored diamonds on chemical containers and doors warn people of the most severe chemical hazards in the chemical containers or in areas such as classrooms. These diamonds were designed by the National Fire Protection Association (NFPA) (See the figure on the following page.). The diamonds designate the following:

❑ health hazards (left, blue diamond)

❑ fire hazards (top, red diamond)

❑ instability or reactivity hazards (right, yellow diamond)

❑ special information (bottom, white diamond)

A number code representing the severity of the hazard is given in the blue, red, and yellow diamonds. The numbers range from zero to four, with zero indicating no hazard and four indicating a severe hazard. The special information diamond indicates special warnings, such as reactivity with water and corrosiveness.

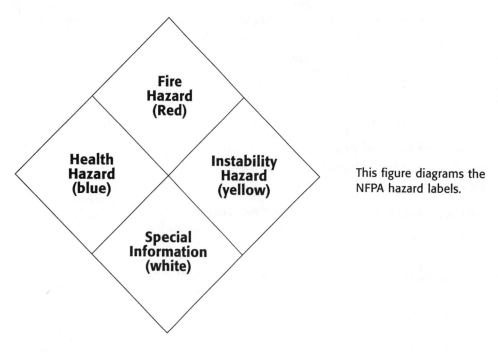

This figure diagrams the NFPA hazard labels.

The lack of labeling or improper labeling may cause you or your students to use incompatible chemicals together and may result in disaster. In addition, improper labeling is one of the most cited (and most looked for) violations by OSHA inspectors. You may wonder if temporary storage is exempt. Laboratory Safety Standard states that temporary containers (for example, beakers and flasks) of chemicals intended for immediate use need not be labeled. However, OSHA inspectors have issued citations when such containers were observed unattended. In general, you must ensure that labels are present and intact, are not defaced or illegible, and are prominently displayed.

The Laboratory Safety Standard also requires suppliers to provide a legible label for every chemical purchased. Every shipment should be immediately inspected, and any containers that have unreadable labels should be returned to the supplier. Labels should contain the following information:

❑ name of the chemical (not a formula)

❑ appropriate hazard warnings

❑ name and address of the supplier

❑ date on which the chemical was received (date on which the chemical was opened or date by which the chemical should be disposed of is also recommended)

❑ the chemical abstract number, if possible

Labels do not pertain only to chemical bottles. Signs should be posted to designate locations of safety equipment and to indicate specific hazards or hazardous areas. Exits in your classroom should already be marked. However, below is a list of tips to think about when addressing labels.

✔ Use the standard signs developed for special hazards (for example, lasers and fire hazards).

✔ Post specific warning signs for hazards found in activities. Warnings should also be included in instructional materials.

✔ Extinguishers' signs should clearly indicate the type of fire for which the extinguishers are intended; do not assume that everyone knows the meanings of Class A, B, C or D fires or fire extinguishers.

✔ Waste containers must be clearly labeled with the type of waste product intended for them.

✔ Make sure that everyone can see the signs. If people are not able to see the signs, inform them of where equipment and exits are.

Wear protection during experiments

The Laboratory Safety Standard requires that personal protective equipment be worn by people handling hazardous chemicals or by people who are in proximity to hazardous chemicals. The personal protective equipment should correspond to the potential hazards of chemicals used in experiments and could include eye, face, hand, body, foot, head, and respiratory protection. The following list describes some protective equipment.

❑ **Eye or face protection** This form of protection should be provided whenever students might be exposed to flying objects or to chemicals. Eye and face protection should conform to document ANSI Z87.1–1989 of the American National Standard Practice for Occupational and Educational Eye and Face Protection. In addition, eyewear must be appropriate for the hazard. For example, goggles used to protect against flying objects usually have side or top vents. These goggles are not appropriate if protection from chemical splashes is needed. Wear goggles, and have your students wear safety goggles for the duration of all experiments.

❑ **Hand protection** Appropriate hand protection must be provided when hands may be exposed to harmful chemicals that can be absorbed by the skin or that can produce chemical burns. Do not assume that because general-purpose gloves offer some hand protection, these gloves protect from all chemicals used in experiments.

❑ **Laboratory coats and aprons** Lab coats or aprons should be provided to protect clothing against spills and splashes.

❑ **Foot protection** Many foot protection requirements of the various safety agencies focus on physical hazards. However, exposed skin on the feet is susceptible to injury if a chemical were spilled on it. So, do not allow students to wear sandals or open-toed shoes during an experiment. Canvas shoes should also be discouraged because they provide feet with little protection from chemicals. Leather shoes or tennis shoes provide enough protection that a person should be able to remove these types of shoes before a chemical spilled on the shoes would affect his or her skin.

❑ **Head protection** Head protection is needed only if a hazard from falling objects is present. Try to eliminate hazards from falling objects in the classroom. This type of hazard may be necessary in some physics experiments (projectile experiments), but the chemistry experiments should be free of such hazards.

❑ **Respiratory protection** This type of protection (for example, half-face masks and self-contained breathing apparatus) should never be necessary in an educational activity. Any activity requiring respiratory protection is inappropriate in the K–12 setting, because the use of this type of protection means that you and your students are dealing with very toxic and very volatile chemicals. In addition, requirements for respiratory protection are too individualized and are too difficult to provide for this setting.

Students and teachers should wear the proper protective equipment when performing an experiment.

Use and maintain safety equipment

The Laboratory Safety Standard also requires you to have safety equipment in your classroom. Your chemical hygiene plan should detail what safety equipment is in your classroom and how the equipment is to be maintained. The following list provides useful details about some safety equipment.

❏ **Eyewash** An eyewash station should be located as close as possible to the laboratory benches (no more than 25 ft or 10 seconds away) so that an injured person can easily access the eyewash. In addition, the water in your eyewash station should be able to run freely after the eyewash is turned on. The eyewash station should also be sufficient to allow a person to bathe both eyes at a rate of 0.4 gal/min with 16°C–32°C (60°F–90°F) water for at least 15 minutes. At least one eyewash station in your classroom should be ADA compliant. Flush eyewash stations for 5 minutes every week to rid the eyewash of dirt and bacteria.

❏ **Safety shower** A safety shower should be located as close as possible to the laboratory benches (no more than 50 ft or 10 seconds away), and the water from the shower should be able to run freely after the shower is turned on. The safety shower must also be sufficient to flush affected tissue at a rate of 20 gal/min (at 30 psi) with 16°C–32°C (60°F–90°F) water. The shower should be large enough to accommodate at least

 SAFETY SUGGESTIONS

Flushing eyewash stations and safety showers weekly may seem like a nuisance, but imagine you have just been splashed with acid. You would not want to rinse your possibly damaged eyes and skin with dirty, stagnant water.

Eyewash stations must be accessible to all students and teachers.

CHAPTER 5

two people under the shower head. The safety shower should be ADA compliant as well. Rid your showers of dirt and bacteria by flushing them every week.

❑ **Fume hoods** There should be at least one fume hood per classroom and one fume hood per preparatory room. Each fume hood should have an air-face velocity of at least 60 ft/min. Prepare chemicals in your fume hood and allow your students to work in and become familiar with a fume hood, especially if your students are working with flammable, toxic, or odorous gases.

❑ **Fire extinguishers** Use a fire extinguisher only if you believe the fire can be extinguished and you have been trained to use an extinguisher. Do not waste time that you could use to get out of the burning classroom by trying to extinguish a fire. You should have a fire extinguisher that can extinguish at least A, B, and C classes of fires.

 SAFETY SUGGESTIONS

If your safety showers were installed without a drain, use this method to flush your showers. Suspend a shower curtain around each shower and funnel the water into a large bucket so that the amount of water spilled on the floor is reduced.

 **SAFETY SUGGESTIONS**

Most local fire departments will visit your school and train you and other staff to use fire extinguishers.

 SAFETY INFORMATION

Class of fire	Type of fire extinguisher
A Fire produced from materials such as wood, cloth, paper, rubber, and plastics	water and halogenated hydrocarbon extinguishers
B Fire produced from flammable liquids and gases common to most laboratories	carbon dioxide, dry powder, and halogenated hydrocarbon extinguishers
C Fire produced by electrical equipment and instruments	carbon dioxide, dry powder, and halogenated hydrocarbon extinguishers
D Fire produced by combustible metals	Met-L-X

❑ **Safety ladder** Safety ladders are more stable than regular ladders—safety ladders do not slip or collapse.

❑ **Safety blankets** Safety blankets can be used to extinguish a fire on a person. However, a safety shower is preferable to a safety blanket for extinguishing a fire on a person because a shower extinguishes the fire faster than a blanket does and a blanket holds in heat. A safety blanket can also be a handy tool for quickly containing a spill or fire while you are evacuating your classroom.

 SAFETY SUGGESTIONS

Regularly conduct a check of safety equipment. The right time to determine the locations and the effectiveness of your safety equipment is not during in an accident. Anticipate what could go wrong in every experiment, and create a plan to use safety equipment effectively during accidents.

Store your chemicals safely

One of the safest approaches to storing chemicals is to avoid excessive inventories. Store the smallest amounts of chemicals possible, because smaller amounts of chemicals create fewer hazards than larger amounts of chemicals do. Listed below are some ways to ensure that only the necessary amounts of chemicals are in your storeroom.

✔ Order only the chemicals necessary to complete the experiments you have planned. Do not order in bulk. The apparent cost savings are easily outweighed by the potential costs of increased hazards and of disposal.

✔ Reevaluate your experiments to ensure that excess chemicals are not used to complete experiments.

✔ Run experiments on a small-scale or microscale basis.

Never store chemicals alphabetically. Storing chemicals alphabetically places incompatible chemicals in close proximity to each other and creates the potential for disastrous results. Chemicals can be segregated into two areas designated for

❑ flammables

❑ nonflammables/combustibles

(You should not have any pyrophoric or unstable chemicals in your classroom.)

 SAFETY SUGGESTIONS

For a list of incompatible chemicals, refer to *Prudent Practices for the Disposal of Hazardous Chemicals*, by the Committee on Hazardous Substances in the Laboratory, the Commission on Physical Sciences, Mathematics, and Resources, and the National Research Council.

CHAPTER 5

Safe storage of chemicals also requires appropriate facilities. An appropriate chemical storage area should have the following characteristics:

✔ The chemical storage area should be separate from the laboratory area but should be close enough so that you can easily distribute chemicals.

✔ The storeroom should be easy to evacuate in an emergency. However, access to the storeroom should be limited to qualified persons only.

✔ The storage area should be separated by a firewall from neighboring rooms or hallways and should have a fire-resistant floor and a fire-resistant ceiling, if appropriate.

✔ The storage area should have a ventilation system that vents air from the storeroom to the outside of the building and that produces 4 to 12 changes of air per hour. Exhaust fans are recommended to remove smoke and vapors.

✔ Certain chemicals may corrode and damage the storage area, so use cupboards, cabinets, and shelves that are made of materials that are not reactive with the chemicals being stored on them. (For example, metal corrodes easily in the presence of acids so avoid metal shelves and cabinets to store acids.)

Listed below are some tips about storing chemicals that will be used in your classroom experiments.

✔ Only essential amounts of chemicals should be stored in the laboratory itself, and they should be stored only for as long as they are needed for a particular activity.

✔ Shelves in the chemical storeroom should not be mounted too high on walls, even if steps or ladders are provided. It is too easy to drop a container or lose one's balance while climbing.

✔ Shelves should be mounted securely to the wall and should have lips so that containers cannot easily drop from the edge.

✔ In areas that have earthquakes, chemicals may need to be secured to shelves rather than just placed on shelves.

✔ Liquid and solid chemicals should be segregated.

✔ Chemicals should be segregated according to their compatibility with water. Additional segregation of chemicals may be necessary if chemicals are too toxic or too reactive to be stored on an open shelf or with other chemicals.

 **DID YOU KNOW?**

Acetone is incompatible with concentrated sulfuric acid, mercury and halogens are incompatible with ammonia, and alkali and alkaline earth metals are incompatible with water.

✔ Do not overload shelves. Containers may fall off of an over-loaded shelf and break when you try to move them to get to another container. Even worse, overloaded shelves may collapse.

✔ Liquids should be placed on chemically resistant trays to contain moderate leaks and spills.

✔ Liquids should be stored close to the floor, especially if they are in glass containers.

✔ A spill cleanup kit should be easily accessible in the chemical storage area.

✔ Do not store chemical waste in the same area in which usable chemicals are stored.

✔ Secondary containers should be available for transporting and dispensing chemicals.

✔ Carts for transporting chemicals should have deep trays so that containers cannot slide off.

Store and dispose of waste appropriately

Waste can be hazardous. OSHA provides regulations for storage and disposal of waste. An effective way of handling chemical waste is to have the smallest amount possible of each chemical in your class-room. Waste is also reduced through careful planning. Each activity should be mapped out so that only necessary chemicals and the necessary amounts of these chemicals are used. Listed below are several questions to guide you in eliminating chemical waste and hazards.

❑ Are the facilities available for use suitable for the activity under consideration?

❑ Can less hazardous chemicals be substituted for more hazardous chemicals?

❑ Are minimum quantities of the required chemicals being ordered?

❑ Are only the minimum quantities of chemicals used during experiments?

❑ Is sufficient and appropriate storage available for all of the required chemicals?

❑ Can any chemicals be recycled?

❑ Can any chemicals be disposed of in the classroom by using an accepted standard laboratory procedure?

❑ Are any unusual disposal requirements necessary?

CHAPTER 5

In addition, here are some tips that will help you eliminate chemical waste and hazards.

✔ **Reduce the scale of experiments.**

    ✔ Only the minimum amount of each chemical should be used.

    ✔ Use microscale techniques during experiments to reduce chemical usage.

    ✔ Whenever possible, substitute newer, more sensitive equipment that effectively uses smaller amounts of chemicals.

✔ **Store waste appropriately.**

    ✔ Do not allow unused chemicals to accumulate.

    ✔ Regularly check short shelf-life chemicals for deterioration; dispose of chemicals before they decompose into more-hazardous forms.

    ✔ Avoid purchasing large quantities of chemicals for the volume discount—short-term savings may be easily outstripped by disposal costs.

    ✔ Always put the date you received the chemical or an expiration (disposal) date on the chemical label.

    ✔ Consider the waste's reactivity and hazards while storing the waste in containers.

    ✔ Take care to segregate potentially incompatible classes of wastes; some chemical wastes cannot be stored together because they react dangerously.

    ✔ After waste is placed in a secure and properly labeled container, take the waste to the designated storage area. Waste should not be stored in the chemical storage area.

    ✔ Do not store waste for more than 90 days.

✔ **Maintain labels.**

    ✔ Ensure that all containers have appropriate labels.

SAFE LABS

Although large amounts of chemicals are traditionally used to ensure that better quantitative results are obtained, consider identifying a few key experiments in which very accurate qualitative results are needed. Many activities can still be meaningful when performed with a qualitative emphasis.

DID YOU KNOW?

When ethers or ether solutions evaporate, they may leave peroxides. These peroxides are hazardous because they are explosive. Even the minor shock of unscrewing the cap on a container of peroxide can cause these chemicals to detonate. If you suspect you have these substances in your storeroom, contact organizations that are trained to deal with them such as a police bomb squad or your waste disposal company.

✔ Waste container labels are somewhat different from chemical package labels; one must provide enough information on the waste container labels to ensure safe handling and disposal. Waste labels should include the following:

❑ chemical names of the principal components and of minor components that may be hazardous

❑ initial date of accumulation

❑ appropriate hazard category (for example, toxic and corrosive)

✔ Periodically check the condition of labels; replace those beginning to loosen or to deteriorate. Laboratory analysis of unknown chemicals is expensive.

✔ Always put the date you received the chemical or an expiration (disposal) date on the chemical label.

✔ **Establish an exchange program.**

✔ Develop a trade program with colleagues at neighboring schools or businesses. Surplus chemicals can be swapped for needed ones.

Be very careful about disposing chemicals. Removal and final disposition of hazardous waste should be performed by chemical disposal companies. They can also ensure that waste is properly packaged and labeled according to Department of Transportation guidelines. Small amounts of some nontoxic water-soluble chemicals can be discarded into a sanitary sewer system, but never into a storm sewer system. Storm sewer systems empty into untreated bodies of water.

Good sense is required when you dispose of chemicals. In many school facilities, a common practice is to interconnect sink drains from various areas. Therefore, vapors from substances poured down one sink may emerge from another. Substances disposed in different sinks may also react when they come in contact with each other. Substances that smell bad should not be disposed in the sink.

 SAFETY INFORMATION

Facts on chemicals that can be discarded in a sanitary sewer system and other useful waste disposal information are listed in the book *Prudent Practices for the Disposal of Hazardous Chemicals,* by the Committee on Hazardous Substances in the Laboratory, the Commission on Physical Sciences, Mathematics, and Resources, and the National Research Council.

CHAPTER 5

Oops! What do I do if a chemical spill occurs?

In the event of a hazardous spill, first assist anyone who was contaminated by treating the person at an eyewash station, in a safety shower, or through another appropriate means and then warn those nearby of the spill. Do not bother to wipe or rinse out contaminated clothing—quickly remove all contaminated clothing and flush chemicals from skin and other affected areas for at least 15 minutes. Modesty about removing clothes should be disregarded when personal safety is threatened. Temporary embarrassment may be worth enduring to prevent months of painful injury and recovery. No one should be allowed in the area of the spill. Depending on the extent and nature of the chemical spill, evacuation may be necessary.

After all individuals receive the necessary treatment after a spill, follow the tips below to help you clean up a chemical spill.

 SAFETY INFORMATION

Do not pour water into concentrated acid, such as concentrated sulfuric acid. Pour the concentrated acid into water to avoid any spattering of liquid or breakage of glass due to energy generated from the reaction of water and the acid.

✔ Appropriate protective apparel must be worn while cleaning up the spill.

✔ Dispose of the chemical spill in an appropriate manner. One task often forgotten is cleaning the contaminated area after the spilled material has been removed. Remember to clean nearby equipment and bottles that may have been contaminated. Don't forget: Most spills on floors also splash on nearby surfaces, such as cabinets, walls, and counter tops.

✔ Spills of hazardous solid materials can be gently swept into a dustpan and discarded appropriately. More-hazardous materials may require a HEPA-filtered vacuum cleaner.

✔ Liquid spills must be contained as quickly as possible. Small amounts can be absorbed by a neutralizer (if an acid or base spill) or by an inert material. Large spills—or spills of very hazardous materials—should be handled by professional hazardous materials teams.

✔ Spill cleanup kits may be purchased from any laboratory safety reseller. Kits can also be assembled locally. They should contain the following:

   ✔ absorbents (sand, kitty litter, or vermiculite)

   ✔ neutralizers (sodium carbonate or sodium bisulfite)

   ✔ dust pan and brush (obtain a set that can be used only for spill cleanup)

   ✔ disposal bags and containers, various sizes (with blank labels)

✔ paper towels and sponges (use with caution)

✔ gloves

✔ goggles

✔ an apron or a coat

 DID YOU KNOW?

Mercury and Containing Mercury Spills

Mercury spills were once a common laboratory accident because many thermometers and vacuum system equipment contained mercury. No matter how well these accidents were cleaned, some mercury usually remained. Pouring unwanted mercury down the sink was also not uncommon during these accidents. While the use of mercury in instruments has decreased in recent years, mercury is still found in many classrooms. The occurrence of mercury in classrooms is hazardous because the chronic breathing of mercury vapor leads to mercury poisoning, which affects the nervous system primarily. However, commercially available mercury cleanup kits usually have a chemical that, when sprinkled over the mercury with a little water, amalgamates with the mercury for easier cleanup.

CHAPTER 5

Noise Hazards

What are noise hazards?

Every day we encounter sounds that annoy us, that interfere with our hearing and communication, or that may be hazardous to our health. Any such unwanted sounds are called **noise.** Note the subjectivity involved in this definition—what is noise to one person may not be noise to another. Despite the subjectivity in this definition of noise, excessive exposure to noise can be harmful.

DEFINITIONS

noise
any unwanted sound or sounds

Noise is often thought of in terms of magnitude. Many people think of noise as a loud sound occurring in a relatively short period of time. However, some low-intensity, continuous sounds can also match the definition of noise. There are four types of noise:

❑ **Continuous** Noise is continuous if the magnitude of the noise does not vary over time.

❑ **Intermittent** Noise is intermittent if the noise stops and starts at intervals.

❑ **Impulsive** Noise is impulsive if the noise is large in magnitude but short in duration.

❑ **Varying** Noise is varying if the magnitude of the noise changes over time.

What are the effects of noise?

Exposure to noise can cause short-term or long-term harm to people. You may be at greater risk of the harmful effects of noise than your students are because students may be exposed to the harmful noise during only one class period, but you may be exposed to noise all day. Noise can cause hearing loss, speech interference, lack of concentration, and annoyance. Listed below are detailed descriptions of these effects.

❑ **Hearing loss** Hearing loss is the most studied effect of noise exposure and is well documented. The potential for a person to experience hearing loss due to a given noise is determined by the total sound pressure level of the noise, the frequency dependence of the noise's energy, the time distribution of the exposure to the noise, and the susceptibility of the individual to noise-induced hearing loss. Understanding that hearing loss can affect people of any age is important.

Short exposures to loud noise can cause temporary hearing loss, which is called *auditory fatigue.*

Loud sounds can also damage the hair cells and nerve endings in the cochlea. (See the figure below for a diagram of the ear.) Damage to the cochlea or any part of the inner ear often leads to permanent hearing loss. Permanent hearing loss can be cumulative if exposure to the noise is prolonged or repeated. In addition, permanent hearing loss often occurs over a long period of time and can be difficult to identify in the early stages. One of the most common types of hearing loss is called **tinnitus.**

 DEFINITIONS

tinnitus
a common type of hearing loss in which affected people hear ringing in their ears and have trouble understanding other people and hearing the difference between words that sound similar

❑ **Speech interference** Noise does not have to produce hearing loss to disrupt communication. Loud noises will prevent people from hearing each other. Fatigue and vocal problems can result from people constantly yelling over this type of noise.

❑ **Lack of concentration** Excessive classroom noise will cause students to have difficulty concentrating during class. Studies have shown that academic performance of students in quiet classrooms surpasses the academic performance of students in noisy classrooms. Evidence also suggests that noisy classrooms promote student aggression.

 SAFETY INFORMATION

Read the book *Nonauditory Effects of Noise on Behavior and Health* by Cohen and Weinstein for more information about the effects of noise on academic performance.

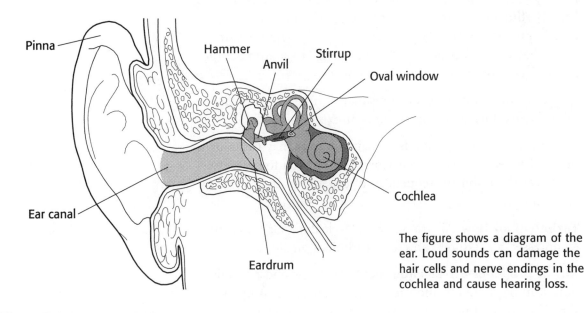

The figure shows a diagram of the ear. Loud sounds can damage the hair cells and nerve endings in the cochlea and cause hearing loss.

CHAPTER 6

❑ **Annoyance** Annoyance is a common reaction to noise. People have different levels of tolerance to noise. A group's level of tolerance to noise is based on individual tolerance, any unpleasantness associated with the noise, and on the appropriateness of the noise to the noise-producing activity.

In an educational setting, one seldom encounters noise at a level sufficient to cause immediate hearing loss. Most hearing loss that results from noise in a classroom occurs over a long period of time. Noises that disrupt, distract, or annoy you or your students are more immediate concerns. These noises may cause students to be inattentive to their experiments or to your instruction. Such inattentiveness can create safety hazards. Safety problems can also develop if students cannot understand your instructions or cannot hear sounds that indicate equipment is malfunctioning.

What are sources of noise in the classroom?

An obvious source of noise is rowdy students bustling into your classroom before the tardy bell rings. Noise also comes from equipment during experiments. In addition, noise can come from a variety of less obvious sources:

❑ **Vibrating solids and air columns** The sources of vibrating solids may be sorted into two categories: instructional and facility. Some examples of instructional sources are speakers or membranes, mechanical oscillators, and wave generators. Facility sources are things such as tabletops or support rods. Facility sources vibrate because of the operation of instructional apparatus. Other facility sources may be windows or ducts that vibrate because of the operation of vacuum equipment or window air conditioning units.

Vibrating air columns occur in resonance tubes or musical instruments during demonstrations or experiments.

The effects of vibrating solids and air columns may be amplified if the frequencies of their vibrations happen to be at or very near the resonant frequencies of other vibrating solids or air columns.

❑ **Turbulent air flow** Air tracks or tables, leaking air hoses, or compressed air fixtures can create turbulent air flow.

❑ **Air- or propeller-driven equipment** Air noise and propeller noise can be caused by motors, blowers, fans, and compressors. This type of noise can easily be transmitted through ducts and may create low-pitched vibrations in these ducts. Ducts that are attached to hoods are especially prone to vibration. Aging air supply units for air tracks and tables may also generate this type of noise.

❑ **Explosions** Explosions, which are rapid changes in temperature or pressure, ususally generate noise. Bursting gas-filled
balloons, erupting chemical reactions, and breaking wine
glasses are examples of explosions that are the intentional
result of some demonstrations.

Activities that have the potential for explosion should be
planned for very carefully or avoided altogether.

Sound levels are described in decibels.

The ear is sensitive to a wide range of pressure changes or intensities
of sound. The normal range of human hearing is from 2×10^{-5} N/m^2
to 20 N/m^2. It is convenient to express such a wide range in terms of
a logarithmic scale and as a ratio of a measured level to a reference
level. The *decibel* is the unit used to express this ratio of sound pressure levels. The expression to describe sound level is

$$L_p \text{ (in decibels, dB)} = 20 \log P/P_o$$

The reference level P_o value is usually the threshold of
hearing, 2×10^{-5} N/m^2.

Although we tend to think of the decibel as a unit
of measurement, the decibel is a ratio (note the result
of the equation is dimensionless). Values of sound
levels are expressed in terms of *dBA* or *dBC*. The *A*
and *C* of these terms refer to the filter network used
to obtain the values (see the next section).

DID YOU KNOW?

Note that 0 dB does not mean that
there is no sound. It means that the
measured sound level is equal to the
threshold of human hearing. Thus,
having negative sound levels is possible. Sounds at negative levels are
below the threshold of hearing.

How can I measure noise?

A fundamental apparatus for measuring noise is the
sound-level meter. These meters give a single value
for the level of sound measured. More-complex
sounds (for example, sounds that consist of several
tones or that have a continuous spectrum) require
more-complex equipment, such as octave band
analyzers and tape recorders, for analysis. However,
sound-level meters are sufficient for most noise
measurements in the academic setting.

SAFETY INFORMATION

Meters that meet American National
Standards Institute (ANSI) standards
are classified as Type 1 (precision),
Type 2 (general purpose), or Type 3
(survey).

A and C filter networks

The most recently developed sound-level meters have two frequency-
weighted settings called the A and C filter networks. The human ear
responds differently to various frequencies and intensities of sound.
We do not hear very high and very low frequency sounds well. The

function of the A and C filter networks is to compensate for our inability to hear sounds of certain frequencies well. These filter networks standardize (A-weighting or C-weighting) the frequencies that compose each noise to be measured.

❑ The A network simulates the sensitivity of the human ear for frequencies at moderate sound levels (40–85 decibels). The network gives a weighted value for the sound levels of all frequencies that compose the noise to be measured by a meter. The A filter network (A-weighting) is more frequently used than the C filter network (C-weighting).

❑ The C network simulates the sensitivity of the human ear for frequencies at high sound levels (above 85 decibels) and gives a weighted value for the sound levels of all frequencies that compose the noise to be measured by a meter. Because the human ear responds the same to all high sound levels in the audible frequency range, loud sounds do not have to be weighted as much as moderately loud and quiet sounds.

A meter on the A filter network setting would be used to measure the sound level of environmental noise (light-ballast hum or general classroom noise), and a meter on the C filter network setting would be used to measure the sound level of a gas-filled balloon explosion or a loud-speaker. Some meters have a third setting for a flat response network. These meters take nonstandardized measurements of the entire audible frequency range.

> ## ✔ DID YOU KNOW?
>
> | Sound Levels of Common Noises | Sound Pressure Level |
> | --- | --- |
> | Air conditioning in an auditorium | 30 dBA |
> | Copying machine 2 m from source of measurement | 50 dBA |
> | Conversational speech | 60 dBA |
> | School children in noisy cafeteria | 80 dBA |
> | Shouting 1.5 m from source of measurement | 100 dBA |

How can I reduce noise in my classroom?

Noise can be reduced by a combination of environmental controls and personal protection:

✔ Reduce the noise coming from a laboratory equipment source.

  ✔ When using equipment that makes noise, run this equipment for only the necessary amount of time.

  ✔ When doing an experiment in which sound is purposefully produced, use the minimum amplitude necessary for the sound to produce the desired effect.

  ✔ Do not allow pieces of equipment to operate at frequencies that create sympathetic vibrations for more than a few seconds.

 SAFETY INFORMATION

> OSHA recommends that the sound pressure level in your classroom should not be above 90 dBA (slow response) for a duration of 8 hours (the duration that you may spend in your classroom). In addition, the sound pressure level in your classroom should not be above 105 dBA (slow response) for a duration of 1 hour (the duration that your students may spend in your classroom).

✔ Reduce the amount of noise transmitted through building components.

  ✔ Use absorbers or padding to limit the amount of noise transmitted from building components.

  ✔ Inform maintenance personal and administration of noise coming from building components.

✔ Change operating procedures.

  ✔ Find alternative experiments to those experiments that make noise.

  ✔ Wear earplugs, and have students wear earplugs. Note that wearing earplugs could produce more hazards because of the earplugs' ability to impair your hearing and the hearing of your students.

  ✔ Inform administration of the effects of noise in your classroom, and suggest purchasing equipment that can reduce or eliminate noise.

CHAPTER 6

ELECTRICAL HAZARDS

What are electrical hazards?

Electrical hazards are caused by

- ❑ the improper use of machinery or apparatus
- ❑ the improper use of electrical outlets
- ❑ the improper use of electrical equipment, such as cables and power cords
- ❑ the improper maintenance of apparatus, outlets, and electrical equipment

When used or maintained improperly, electrical equipment or devices can overheat or produce electrical fires. Frayed cords or exposed wires can easily electrify you or your students. Examples of particular hazards are

- ❑ apparatus with deteriorated power cord insulation
- ❑ a bent or broken prong on a plug
- ❑ a broken prong on a plug protruding from an outlet
- ❑ an overloaded circuit
- ❑ flammable fumes near electrical apparatus
- ❑ metal tools used near energized conductors
- ❑ dangling jewelry near an energized conductor
- ❑ a circuit that someone is working on with both hands
- ❑ a water spill on electrical equipment

 SAFETY INFORMATION

You may know that the extent of injury caused by an electric shock depends on the magnitude of current. (Current is the movement of charge.) However, remember $\Delta V = IR$. Hence, a circuit that has high voltage is also likely to have a large current. So, the best safety practice is to avoid high-voltage circuits.

Does the type of current matter?

Both **alternating current (AC)** and **direct current (DC)** can produce injury to living tissue and can destroy equipment. However, the AC (60 Hz and 120 V) that U.S. electric companies supply to most electrical outlets disturbs human nerve impulses more readily than DC of the same voltage or AC at other frequencies do because human nerve impulses resonate at approximately 60 Hz. In addition, the DC circuits often used in classroom experiments are relatively harmless. Yet, DC can still be dangerous, and burn hazards are created in many common uses of DC. So, all circuits should be treated cautiously.

 DEFINITIONS

alternating current (AC)
a current in which charge moves in one direction and then in the opposite direction

direct current (DC)
a current in which charge moves in one direction

What are the dangers of electricity to living tissue?

Electrical hazards can burn equipment and cause a fire in your classroom. These hazards can also cause serious injuries to you or your students. Specifically, current passing through a body may produce one or more of the following symptoms:

❑ **Shock** Shock should not be confused with electric shock. Shock is an excitation or disturbance of the normal function of nerves or muscles.

❑ **Involuntary muscle reaction** A person who experiences an electric shock may not be able to control her or his muscles. In addition, muscles that a person normally does not control, such as the heart, may operate abnormally.

❑ **Muscle paralysis** An electric shock may prevent muscles from moving (for example, arm muscles cannot flex) or operating (for example, the heart cannot pump blood).

❑ **Burning of tissue and organs** Tissue and organs may be burned so badly that they hemorrhage.

❑ **Death (electrocution)** Death can result from electrocution, which is caused by electric shock.

 SAFETY INFORMATION

Severe electric shocks may cause internal hemorrhages as well as tissue, nerve, and muscle damage. These injuries are often not visible and may not be obvious to onlookers. In addition, an electric shock is often only the beginning of a chain of events. A person who experiences an electric shock may fall and break a bone or get a cut.

Critical values of current and their corresponding physiological effects

Listed below are the critical values of current and their corresponding physiological effects. These approximate values are based on 60 Hz AC passing through the intact skin for one second.

 **DID YOU KNOW?**

Approximately 109 mA of DC will give a female respiratory arrest and approximately 170 mA of DC will give a male respiratory arrest. In contrast, only 19 mA of 60 Hz AC will cause respiratory arrest in a female, and 30 mA of 60 Hz AC will cause respiratory arrest in a male.

Critical values of 60 Hz AC (mA)		Physiological effects
female	**male**	
0.7	1.1	threshold of sensation
1.2	1.8	threshold of painless shock
11	16	paralysis of voluntary muscles
19	30	respiratory arrest
50	75	ventricular fibrillation—the uncoordinated pumping of the heart chambers such that blood does not flow properly (can be fatal)
4000	4000	cardiac arrest
5000	5000	burns that are severe enough to be fatal

 SAFETY INFORMATION

The critical values of 60 Hz AC and their corresponding physiological effects are taken from "The Effects of Electric Shock on Man" by Charles Dalziel. See the appendix for more information.

How can electric shocks occur?

Most electric shocks are caused when people come in contact with defective power cords or with energized instruments whose cases are removed. A person receives an electric shock when he or she becomes part of a live electric circuit—when current enters the body at one point and exits at a different point. You will receive an electric shock if you are in contact with

❑ both energized receptacle slots of an outlet or power cord wires

❑ one energized wire and a ground

❑ a metallic piece that is in contact with an energized conductor and a ground

When instrument cases are open or electric components are exposed, an electric shock is likely to occur. Always make sure that an instrument is unplugged before you inspect the internal components of an instrument. Furthermore, always have a trained technician repair equipment. Students should never work on instruments that use AC and have exposed internal components.

Note that student-assembled circuits that use low-voltage and relatively safe DC power sources (such as D-cell batteries) are far less hazardous than activities in which AC is used, even though these student circuits are not enclosed in cases. Regardless, remain cautious about students working on electrical devices. (See the sections on resistive heating and on the prevention of electrical hazards.)

 **DID YOU KNOW?**

Capacitors should always be treated with caution because capacitors store charge and can deliver an unexpected electric shock.

What conditions affect the severity of electric shock?

Several factors, in addition to the magnitude and type of current, affect the severity of electric shock. Those factors include the following:

❑ **Current path through the body** Electric shocks are less severe if the current path does not include vital organs.

❑ **Length of time the electric shock acts on the body** The duration of the electric shock effects the extent of injury—the longer the duration of the electric shock on the body, the greater risk of severe injury. In addition, the electric shock can influence the duration of exposure if a victim cannot let go of the conductor of electricity that is causing the electric shock because of loss of voluntary muscle control.

❑ **Location on the body of the electrical contact** An electric shock that starts at a finger and exits through the grounded elbow on the same arm will do less damage than an electric shock that starts at a finger and exits through the victim's grounded feet. The latter scenario is more dangerous because more tissue is affected and the path of current is closer to internal organs.

Current can burn vital organs even if the current does not pass through those vital organs. This type of damage may occur externally because of arcing or thermal contact (a vital organ is near tissue that is experiencing electric shock). The likelihood of this type of damage increases at high current levels.

DID YOU KNOW?

The severity of heart injury that an electric shock can cause depends on which stage of the pumping cycle the heart was in at the instant the electric shock occurred.

❑ **Skin resistance** The resistance of the body greatly affects the severity of the electric shock. Human tissue has very low resistance because the cellular fluid in tissue is a good conductor of electricity. However, dry skin has very high resistance—approximately a hundred thousand ohms ($10^5\Omega$). Resistance of wet skin is low—a thousand ohms or less ($10^3\Omega$). Skin resistance is even lower than the resistance of wet skin if a cut or deep abrasion is present. The exposure of moist and deeper skin layers increases the severity of injury that results from the electric shock.

Because low resistance results in high current for a given potential difference $(I = \Delta V/R)$, the current in wet skin can be several hundred times greater than the current in dry skin. Whether you have wet or dry skin can mean the difference between a harmless electric shock and an electric shock that causes serious burns and interferes with the functions of internal organs.

❑ **Other physiological and psychological factors** Age and physical condition affect the severity of an electric shock. Body resistance also varies according to muscular structure.

Studies show that for a given current, a person concentrating on a task may not experience the same electric shock as a person who is daydreaming and then is startled when the electric shock occurs.

What should I do if someone is electrified?

If someone is electrified, tell a student to get another teacher to call for emergency personnel. Then, remove the person from contact with the energized conductor. Do not try to touch the person or you may be electrified as well. You can turn off the power of the device that is causing the electric shock if this can be done safely (for example, turning off the circuit breaker for the outlet in which the device is plugged). Or you can obtain an insulator, such as a wooden meterstick, and break the contact between the person who is being electrified and the energized conductor.

After the person who is suffering from electric shock has been removed from the source of the shock, check to see if this person is having breathing problems or is experiencing ventricular fibrillation. Artificial respiration or cardiopulmonary resuscitation should be performed on the person who experienced electric shock, if necessary. Also, use blankets to keep the person warm. Although a person who is electrified may appear unharmed, call emergency personnel because this person may have suffered internal injuries, such as burns to organs during the electric shock.

What is resistive heating?

Resistive heating is the thermal energy that current produces while moving through circuits. This type of energy is also known as *Joule heating* or I^2R *loss* and can be a hazard to you, your students, and your equipment. Charges colliding with (instead of moving smoothly through) atoms or ions of the conductor can produce resistive heating. When such collisions occur, the charges lose kinetic energy, but the conductor gains thermal energy. Resistive heating can occur if

DEFINITIONS

resistive heating
the heating of electrical components due to the passage of current

- ❑ equipment components or conductors are not rated for the amount of current in their circuit

- ❑ outlets or circuits are overloaded

- ❑ electrical connections are poorly or improperly made

- ❑ apparatus is not properly ventilated

The effects of resistive heating are as follows:

- ❑ burns, if hot components are accidentally touched

- ❑ ignition of combustible materials in the vicinity of equipment that has resistive heating

- ❑ vaporization of or explosion of components

Resistive heating is easy to prevent

Fortunately, resistive heating can be prevented easily by good laboratory technique and proper use of equipment. You should experience little resistive heating if you follow, in order, these simple steps.

- ✔ Before you start building your circuit, plan your circuit by drawing a schematic that identifies all components of the circuit.

✔ Estimate the current that each component of the circuit will have, based on the voltage of the power source.

✔ Compare your estimates of current with the ratings for the components you will use to prevent overloading the components.

✔ Connect all components in the circuit except the power source, and verify that all connections are properly made.

✔ Open the switch or turn the power source off while you connect the power source to the circuit.

✔ Leave the power source on only as long as necessary to perform the desired actions or functions.

✔ Open a switch or turn the power source off as soon as the necessary measurements or observations have been made.

 **SAFETY SUGGESTIONS**

If a fire occurs because of an electrical hazard, try to extinguish the fire only if you believe that you can extinguish the fire safely. Do not use water to extinguish an electrical fire. Use a Class C fire extinguisher.

What are other electrical concerns?

Electric shock and resistive heating are not the only hazards associated with electrical equipment. Charges may move as a current spontaneously. Although these arcs and sparks typically create currents that exist for a short duration, these charges can still be hazardous.

Is static electricity a concern?

Static electricity is caused by an imbalance of electrons between two surfaces. The imbalance can be corrected by transferring electrons from one surface to another surface by conduction or induction. When the excess charge on a surface is discharged, a person standing near the discharge can be electrified. However, these electric shocks are not normally hazardous, so students do not have to report every instance of a shock by static electricity.

One serious concern related to static electricity is the accumulation of static electricity near a hazardous material such as a flammable gas or vapor. Static electricity can cause a flammable gas or vapor to ignite. Another concern is the potential for an injury to result from someone reacting to electric shock by, for example, rapidly pulling her or his hand away and knocking over a beaker.

Are there any other issues I should be concerned about?

You should be concerned about the following:

❏ **Sparks** Sparks are created when electricity jumps across a small gap in a circuit. Many types of electrical equipment are capable of creating sparks—thermostats, drills, and motors commonly produce sparks. Sparks are dangerous because they can ignite flammable materials or shock you or your students.

❑ **Electric arcs** Electric arcs are bands of sparks and may be created when a circuit is shorted, when the flow of a current is interrupted, or even when a switch is closed. Electric arcs are capable of causing electric shocks and combustion of materials. To prevent the occurrence of electric arcs, always ensure that components of circuits are properly connected before energizing the circuits and never close a switch or circuit breaker slowly.

What can I do to prevent electrical hazards?

You can prevent or minimize electrical hazards easily. Listed below are some steps you can take to minimize these hazards.

✔ **Apparatus and Electrical Fixtures**

✔ Often inspect the insulation on power cords, patch cords, and cables for deterioration. If a conductor is exposed, remove it from use or repair it immediately.

✔ Do not splice equipment or cords. Do not use any equipment or cords that have splices.

✔ Always use power cords rated for the device with which they are to be used. Ensure that connecting cords and cables are also rated for the magnitude of the current to be found in an activity.

✔ Never remove the ground prong from a plug. If a plug is missing the ground prong, replace the plug immediately or stop using the apparatus with the broken plug.

✔ Do not use three-to-two prong adapters.

✔ Have any two-prong electrical outlets replaced as soon as possible. Two-prong outlets do not have the ground prong and are more dangerous than the three-prong outlets.

✔ Do not overload circuits. Using extension cords often overloads circuits.

✔ If a prong is broken off in an outlet, make certain the outlet is de-energized before attempting to remove the prong. Do not let students work in the immediate area until the outlet is de-energized and the prong is removed.

✔ Have loose outlets repaired before allowing anyone to use them—they can cause electrical shorts.

✔ Instruct students to report broken or damaged apparatus or fixtures immediately.

✔ Instruct students to warn you immediately if they touch any apparatus and feel a tingling sensation. Remove the suspect apparatus from use in experiments immediately.

✔ When replacing fuses, use only the type specified for the apparatus; do not attempt to substitute fuses whose current or voltage rating is different from the current or rating required.

✔ Never staple or nail power cords, patch cords, and cables, as is commonly done, to get them out of the way of students or equipment. Use cable ties or plastic wire keepers instead.

✔ Never use the power cord to move or carry apparatus.

✔ Provide adequate ventilation for electrical apparatus.

✔ If apparatus are used near chemicals, periodically check that connections and power cords are not degrading because of the chemicals.

✔ Electrical apparatus that must be used in hoods should be built to prevent sparks.

✔ Provide shielding between exposed vacuum tubes or cathode ray tubes and the students, and provide safety goggles to students. These tubes are potential implosion hazards.

✔ **Environmental**

  ✔ Always keep activity areas dry. Have any leaks repaired immediately, or have students work in an alternate area until repairs are made. Do not allow students to bring water bottles or drinks into the lab.

  ✔ Do not use any electrical apparatus near any water sources or around combustible materials. In particular, do not allow power cords or cables to lie under water faucets or in sinks.

  ✔ If you smell gas when you are entering a room, do not turn on the lights (or other electrical apparatus). A spark may be created by turning on any electrical equipment and may cause an explosion if the gas concentration is large.

  ✔ Do not leave windows open where rain may drop on equipment or create puddles on floors or benches.

  ✔ Make sure electrical panels on equipment are closed and latched, especially if they are accessible to students.

  ✔ Ensure that students have adequate lighting to perform activities.

  ✔ When arranging electrical equipment, take into account that not all students are the same height or that some students have visual or mobility impairments.

✔ **Work Practices**

- ✔ Know your limitations—do not attempt to repair apparatus if you are not certain what to do.

- ✔ Get students in the habit of working on energized electrical circuits (DC or AC) with one hand behind their back.

- ✔ Always construct a circuit, and then connect the circuit to the power source. Always disconnect the power source before disassembling the circuit.

- ✔ Always check that circuits are properly connected.

- ✔ Always have one student act as an observer when a group is working on a circuit. Never let any student work alone on a live circuit.

- ✔ Never allow students to wear jewelry, loose clothing, keys on a cord around the neck, or any other dangling conductors near an energized circuit.

- ✔ Never remove power cords, patch cords, and cables by pulling on the wire. Always use the plug or connector.

- ✔ Keep cords and plugs away from areas where they may be stepped on, pinched between objects, or tripped over.

- ✔ Do not use apparatus that have overextended power cords. Replace the power cord with a longer power cord, use closer outlets, or redesign the layout of the activity in the room.

- ✔ Do not store apparatus with the power cord wrapped tightly around it. A tightly wrapped cord adds stress to the cord at the point the cord enters the apparatus case and leads to the deterioration of the cord's insulation.

 ## ACCIDENT SCENARIO

Electrical Plugs

In a chemistry classroom, students are using hot plates to heat solutions. One student wants to move his hot plate to the other side of his laboratory table and tries to unplug his hot plate without first turning off the hot plate. The plug will not separate from the outlet, so the student uses a metal spatula to free the plug from the outlet. The student experiences an electric shock as a result of his actions.

Tips to avoid electrical plug accidents

- ✔ Remind students of safe practices in the classroom, such as turning off electrical equipment before unplugging the equipment.

✔ If possible, do not use metal instruments such as spatulas during experiments that require electrical equipment.

✔ Do not let students move laboratory equipment during an experiment.

✔ Place warning signs and reminders near equipment.

What kind of outlets do I need?

Outlets (receptacles) in your classroom should have the standard three-prong design as shown in the diagram. This design has a ground connection. Plugs and outlets are wired in a standard way:

❑ The short slot of the outlet (black-wired prong on a plug) is the hot connection.

❑ The longer slot of the outlet (longer, white-wired prong on a plug) is the neutral connection.

❑ The round opening of the outlet (green-wired prong on the plug) is the ground.

The potential between the hot connection and the neutral connection is approximately 120 V. The ground connection protects users by ensuring that the equipment is at the same potential as Earth, which is neutral. You will not experience an electric shock if you and the equipment that you touch are at the same potential as Earth. (For apparatus that need 240 V, their cords will have a plug with a third wire at a potential of −120 V.)

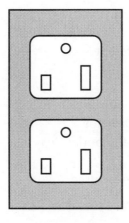

This figure shows a three-prong outlet in the proper orientation.

Receptacles are usually oriented so that the slots form an inverted triangle. This inverted triangle is not the safest arrangement for outlets located on the skirt of the laboratory table because students commonly lean against laboratory tables while they are working. A student may repeatedly lean against a plug, gradually work the plug loose from the receptacle, and partially expose the energized prongs of the plug. A better arrangement in these cases would be to install the outlets as shown in the diagram on the previous page. The first prong to be exposed would be the ground prong, which is not energized (unless there also happens to be a short in the case of the equipment).

Receptacles should be equipped with a ground fault circuit interrupt (GFCI or GFI). Receptacles located near sinks or other water sources must have a GFCI. Receptacles for hoods should be located outside the hoods. This placement prevents ignition of vapors that may be present in the hood because of a plug sparking while being inserted or removed from an outlet.

If there are absolutely no other outlet alternatives and adapters must be used to connect three-prong plugs to a two-prong outlet, be certain to connect the ground on the adapter to a grounded screw on the outlet plate (or other suitable ground). Make sure the outlet panel screw is actually grounded, however. Also ensure that the ground wire is insulated, because if the wire is not truly a ground wire, someone could unknowingly touch it and receive an electric shock.

Dangers of using too much equipment with too few outlets

Receptacles must never be overloaded. Overheating of outlets may cause a fire, especially if combustible material is near the overloaded outlet. To ensure that an outlet is not overloaded, perform the following steps:

✔ Calculate the total load on the outlet or on the entire circuit from the wattage ratings for each device plugged into the outlet or for each component in the circuit.

✔ If the sum of the currents exceeds the current rating (the circuit breaker or fuse rating) for that outlet or circuit, then some devices or equipment must be moved to different outlets.

Do not use multiple outlet plugs that allow more than one apparatus to be plugged into an outlet simultaneously. If you are not careful about what equipment is plugged into the outlet, the outlet may overload and create a serious fire hazard.

For the following reasons, extension cords should never be used.

❏ Although extension cords are intended for temporary use, they have a tendency to become permanent.

❏ Extension cords are fire hazards because they are typically overloaded.

❏ The wires in extension cords are often not rated for their applied loads.

❏ These cords are trip hazards.

THERMAL HAZARDS

What are thermal hazards?

Thermal hazards are objects or substances that transfer energy as **heat.** An open flame is an example of a thermal hazard because it transfers energy to the surroundings as heat. Substances or materials that release heat are contact and fire hazards. In addition, some cold substances will absorb so much heat that they can be thermal hazards. Dry ice and liquid nitrogen are such thermal hazards. Substances or materials that absorb heat are only contact hazards.

What types of thermal hazards exist?

High-temperature thermal hazards are more common in the classroom than thermal hazards that absorb heat. In fact, many experiments and types of equipment release heat intentionally. However, these experiments or types of equipment can release dangerous amounts of heat if they are improperly executed or if they experience mechanical failure. Some obvious examples of thermal hazards are

- ❏ open flames
- ❏ boiling liquids
- ❏ red-hot coils

Other examples of thermal hazards, which may not be obvious, are

- ❏ equipment that is indirectly heated by other equipment
- ❏ exposed light bulbs
- ❏ metal housing on equipment
- ❏ heat sinks
- ❏ combustible products

What effects do thermal hazards produce?

The severity of an injury due to a thermal hazard depends on the

- ❏ source intensity
- ❏ contact time
- ❏ specific heat of the affected tissue

DEFINITIONS

heat
energy transferred from one substance or object to another because of a temperature difference between the substances or objects

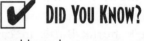

DID YOU KNOW?

A thermal hazard may create another hazard, such as an electrical hazard or a chemical hazard. Thermal hazards may also create an explosion or an implosion.

SAFETY INFORMATION

Energy is transferred as heat through three processes, which are

- ❏ **Conduction** This process is energy moving through a substance or between substances in contact due to a temperature gradient. Thermal hazards created by conduction are probably the most common thermal hazards in your classroom.

- ❏ **Convection** Convection is the transfer of thermal energy by movement of a fluid due to a difference in density between the fluid and another fluid, which is produced by a temperature gradient.

- ❏ **Radiation** In context of this manual, radiation is heat released by a substance through the air or other surrounding gas.

All thermal hazards (whether the hazard is cold or hot) can result in cell death, and eyes or other sensitive areas are more prone to damage by thermal hazards than other areas are. However, injuries from thermal hazards that release heat (hot thermal hazards) can differ from thermal hazards that absorb heat (cold thermal hazards). The next two sections describe both types of injuries and explain how to treat these injuries.

What types of injuries do hot thermal hazards produce?

Burns are the injuries that hot thermal hazards can cause, and skin is the part of the body that is the most susceptible to burns. Burns are categorized as first, second, or third degree. However, burn injuries can be combinations of all three types of burns.

❑ First-degree burns are superficial but can be painful because these burns usually do not damage the nerves. These types of burns will cause outer layers of skin to redden or discolor and to swell slightly.

❑ Second-degree burns penetrate skin more deeply and are more severe than first-degree burns. In addition, second-degree burns affect skin by creating a red or mottled appearance, blisters, and swelling. These burns are also very painful because the nerve endings are still intact.

❑ Third-degree burns are the most severe burns and have the deepest penetration of the types of burns. Third-degree burns may appear white or charred. They may even look like second-degree burns but they extend through all skin layers. In addition, third-degree burns destroy nerve endings, so third-degree burns can be less painful than second-degree burns.

The following table provides the durations of contact that skin can endure with a thermal hazard at specific temperatures before injury results.

Temperature	Time before injury
Up to 44°C (111 °F)	Up to 6 hours
47°C (117 °F)	45 minutes (all layers of skin destroyed)
70°C (158°F)	2 seconds (all layers of skin destroyed)

 DID YOU KNOW?

The properties of a thermal hazard can affect the severity of the injury. For example, boiling water can move more quickly down an arm than a more viscous liquid can. Therefore, the boiling water burns more skin than the viscous liquid. Another example is a substance that has enough thermal energy to eject particles. These particles may become embedded in human tissue.

 DID YOU KNOW?

Although you may think that clothing provides protection from hot liquids and projectiles, clothing can prolong contact with the thermal hazard if the clothing catches fire or absorbs hot liquids.

 SAFETY INFORMATION

The information in the table is taken from *Laboratory Safety: Principles and Practices*, Brinton Miller, ed. See the appendix for more information.

Burns must be treated by medical personnel. However, you or your students may need to provide first aid. Therefore, you should be aware of how to treat a burn until professional help arrives. Listed below are several actions that you can take if someone is burned in your classroom.

✔ Cool minor burns with water.

✔ Refrain from applying ice to any but the most minor first-degree burns.

✔ Refrain from breaking open blisters.

✔ Refrain from touching a burned area because touching the burned area increases the risk of infection.

✔ Refrain from applying ointment to a severe burn.

✔ Refrain from removing anything stuck to a burned area.

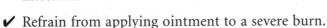 **DEFINITIONS**

burn
destruction of a substance by heat, chemicals, electricity, or radiation

What types of injuries do cold thermal hazards produce?

Cold thermal hazards probably will not produce many injuries in your classroom. However, **frostbite** is the injury most likely to result from contact with cold thermal hazards such as liquid nitrogen. Frostbite is dangerous because it can result in damage to cell structure and cell organs, in protein denaturation, and in the dehydration of cells as well as in other types of damage. The severity of damage to body tissue depends on how long an area is frozen and if the area experiences refreezing. In addition, injuries such as gangrene and capillary and vessel collapse can occur as frozen tissue thaws.

Frostbite must also be treated by medical personnel. However, the best treatment for frostbite until professional help arrives is the rapid rewarming of affected tissue with 32.2°C–41.1°C (90°F–106°F) water. Do not try to keep the affected area frozen or use excessive heat (greater than 48.8°C [120°F]). These techniques produce more tissue damage and possibly burns.

 **DEFINITIONS**

frostbite
injury that results when body tissue releases heat and is frozen

How can I prevent accidents involving thermal hazards?

You can use many methods to prevent or minimize thermal hazards. Such methods are listed below.

✔ Frequently remind students of particular thermal hazards in your classroom, especially the hazards that are not obvious.

✔ Use shields for thermal hazards (or do not remove shields that are provided by the manufacturer).

✔ Maximize the distance between students and hazards.

CHAPTER 8

✔ Provide appropriate protective apparatus and apparel, such as tongs, heat-resistant gloves, and shielded clamps.

✔ Always have students wear goggles during experiments that have thermal hazards.

✔ Make sure notebooks, manuals, and papers are kept away from heat sources.

✔ Arrange gas supply hoses and power cords so that they do not become tangled and cause apparatus to become unstable.

✔ Make sure that cords and hoses do not contact hot or cold equipment.

✔ Always allow sufficient time for all parts of apparatus to cool or warm before touching them. This procedure should be used for parts that are indirectly or directly heated or cooled.

✔ Use the smallest feasible container for boiling.

✔ Never completely fill beakers or other containers with water (or other liquid) if these containers are going to be heated or cooled.

✔ Remember that hot glassware does not look any different from cold glassware.

 **SAFE LABS**

Students are notorious for acting unwisely near thermal hazards. Listed below are some additional tips to help you avoid accidents with thermal hazards.

✔ To prevent students from retrieving samples by reaching into beakers filled with boiling water, use containers that have openings too small for hands to fit into.

✔ During experiments that have thermal hazards, never have containers available that will melt or crack in response to large temperature changes.

✔ Use the fewest heat sources that will allow your class to perform experiments efficiently.

What heat sources are available?

The most common and practical heat sources in your classroom are gas or Bunsen burners, alcohol lamps, and hot plates. Other heat sources that are used include canned heat sources (for example, Sterno or similar solid fuels), compressed gases, heat mantles and tapes, and steam baths. Each of these heat sources has its disadvantages. Some of the disadvantages for gas burners, alcohol lamps, and hot plates are listed below.

Problems with gas burners include the following:

❑ cracked gas supply hoses

❑ obstructed barrels or clogged needle valves (This problem may be caused by melting low temperature objects over the barrel.)

❑ improperly functioning air ports or needle valves

❑ blowback (The gas inside the barrel is ignited.)

❑ difficulty in lighting (Gas flow is too low or too high.)

❑ tangled hoses, which can unbalance the burner

❑ gas supplies that are open even though the burners are out

❑ flames that are difficult to see

Problems with alcohol lamps include the following:

❑ cracked glass, which allows alcohol to leak

❑ spilled alcohol on the outside of the lamp or in the work area

❑ caps on the lamps screwed on improperly

❑ homemade wicks

❑ transferring alcohol in the vicinity of open flames

❑ refilling lamps while the lamps are still hot

❑ uncapping lamps while they are lit

❑ alcohol lamps that are easily tipped over

❑ danger of students drinking the alcohol

❑ nail polish near burning lamps (Although nail polish should not be worn around any open flames, alcohol lamps seem to be a special problem because students tend to be more careless around alcohol lamps than around gas burners.)

Problems with hot plates include the following:

❑ exposed coils on some models

❑ difficulty in determining whether covered-coil hot plates are hot

❑ using water or other liquids in the vicinity of electrical outlets

❑ flammables possibly spilled onto hot plates

❑ power cords resting against the plates

Canned heat sources, compressed gases, heat mantles and tapes, and steam baths have disadvantages that should cause you to use them rarely or never. Canned heat sources, such as Sterno, should never be used. These heat sources often burn with an invisible (or nearly so) flame, so students often cannot tell if these heat sources are in use. Compressed gases (for example, propane or acetylene) are inappropriate for and dangerous in instructional settings. Heat tapes,

Figure shows an example of a gas burner.

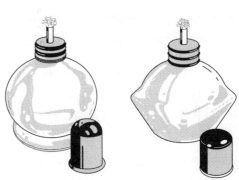

Figure shows examples of alcohol lamps.

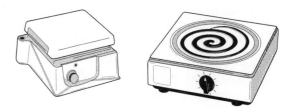

Figure shows examples of hot plates.

CHAPTER 8

heat mantles, and steam baths are usually reserved for specialized tasks and are inappropriate for general heating needs.

How can I avoid accidents while using these heat sources?

Several precautions can prevent accidents with heat sources in general.

- ✔ Heat sources should be carefully inspected before use.

- ✔ All operating parts of heat sources should be functional.

- ✔ Hoses or power cords must not be cracked or deteriorated.

- ✔ Each heat source should be checked to see if it properly operates before students use them.

- ✔ Long hair must be tied back. Baggy clothing and dangling jewelry should not be permitted.

Several ways to avoid accidents when using gas burners are listed below.

- ✔ Make sure nothing obstructs the barrel, needle valve, or gas inlet.

- ✔ Make sure the air port and gas supply valve (if present) operate properly.

- ✔ Make sure the burner is situated so that the hose does not interfere with the stability of the burner.

- ✔ Make sure the burner operates properly.

- ✔ Instruct students in how to properly light and use the burner.

Several ways to avoid accidents when using alcohol lamps include the following:

- ✔ If alcohol lamps must be used, try to use only the tetrahedral-shaped lamps. Cylindrical-shaped lamps tip over too easily. If you must use cylindrical-shaped lamps, try to clamp the lamps in place.

- ✔ Inspect each lamp for cracks, improperly fitting caps, and damaged wicks.

- ✔ Fill lamps before the start of the activity; do not allow students to fill (or refill) lamps.

- ✔ Have extra lamps available to replace empty lamps.

- ✔ Do not keep extra alcohol in the area of the activity.

Accidents that result from the use of hot plates may be avoided if the steps below are followed.

✔ Place hot plates away from water sources.

✔ Place hot plates so the "on" lights can be easily seen by students.

✔ Make sure the cords of hot plates do not interfere with the use of the hot plates and do not contact the hot plates.

In general, hot plates that have covered coils are preferable to gas burners, although burners may be necessary if an experiment requires high heat. Given the large number of anecdotal stories about alcohol lamp accidents compared to experiences in which hot plates or gas burners caused accidents, the use of alcohol lamps is strongly discouraged.

What are some risks of using solder?

Soldering has three areas of risk: thermal hazards, electrical hazards, and flux fumes. Students should not be permitted to solder unsupervised because of the many hazards. Even if students have soldered many times, they must not be allowed to work unsupervised. In addition, soldering should be carried out only by mature students capable of appreciating the risks. Soldering projects that require very high temperatures (for example, silver soldering) should be not be done in your classroom. Given the high degree of supervision required during soldering activities and the often crowded classroom conditions, accidents can easily occur. If you or your students must solder, follow the list below.

✔ Only allow soldering projects that require lower temperature solders.

✔ Provide stands to support soldering irons (pencils). The stands should be the shielded (caged) type, not the small bent wire supports, which do not enclose the tip and heating element.

✔ Provide some type of heat-resistant mat for soldering. The mat protects the tabletop and may prevent the tabletop from catching on fire.

✔ Keep combustible materials out of the soldering area.

✔ Keep students focused on the task. Students talking with neighbors and waving their hands about can easily burn someone or start a fire with solder equipment.

✔ Remind students that the elements and tips may reach temperatures of a few hundred degrees Celsius.

CHAPTER 8

✔ Allow soldering irons or guns sufficient time to cool before touching them.

✔ Do not use soldering equipment near water.

Flux fumes may be a hazard of projects that require a significant amount of soldering. When the flux is heated, fumes containing gaseous and particulate pollutants are produced. These fumes can cause asthma, bronchitis, headaches, dizziness, and shortness of breath. When significant soldering activities are to be performed or if chemically sensitive or allergic people will be soldering, take care that the soldering is done in an open, well-ventilated area or a filtered, portable air extraction system is available.

 **SAFETY SUGGESTIONS**

Soldering by students must be done under the supervision of an experienced adult so that students learn how to solder correctly and safely.

What precautions are necessary for demonstrations that include liquid nitrogen?

Freezing objects in liquid nitrogen is always an exciting activity for students. However, liquid nitrogen is very dangerous and several precautions should be taken to avoid accidents.

✔ Demonstrations that include liquid nitrogen must be carefully planned and performed.

✔ Provide shields between the demonstration and students.

✔ Remind students of the dangers of liquid nitrogen.

✔ Use a container capable of minimizing splashes. Remember that placing warm objects into liquid nitrogen will cause vigorous boiling and splashing.

✔ Be sure to wrap electrical or other heavy-duty tape around "thermos bottle-type" Dewar containers (silvered on the outside) to contain pieces if the containers shatter.

✔ Break items frozen in liquid nitrogen carefully and not where students may try to pick up the pieces. (Demonstrators are often tempted to emphatically break the items they freeze in liquid nitrogen.)

Some teachers have student activities that require the use of liquid nitrogen. These activities are not recommended.

What should I know about glassware?

Materials for activities are often gathered without regard for what glassware should be used. Always take care to use materials appropriate for the potential thermal hazards. In general, cracked or chipped glassware should never be used because such glassware is prone to break. In addition, remember the following rules for using glassware.

✔ When the heating of glassware is necessary, always use borosilicate glass. This glass has a low coefficient of thermal expansion and generally good chemical resistance.

✔ Nevertheless, even this type of glass will break if it is subjected to sudden thermal shocks (drastic changes in temperature).

✔ Always heat glassware slowly, and never place hot glassware on cold or damp surfaces.

✔ Avoid using hot glassware in drafty areas, such as in the vicinity of an operating hood.

✔ Never put liquid nitrogen in glassware.

Are there any specific things to know when heating certain types of glassware?

Specific precautions should be taken when using each type of glassware and each method of heating. A few common precautions are discussed below.

✔ **Test Tubes**

  ✔ Place test tubes in a rack before pouring anything into them.

  ✔ Place the test tube in a test-tube holder before you heat the test tube.

  ✔ Hold the test tube at an angle above the flame. Position the tube so that the flame is directly under the liquid in the tube and is the tube's opening is away from you.

  ✔ Move the test tube slowly above the flame or gently agitate the tube so heat does not build up in one area of the test tube.

  ✔ Never point the open end of the tube at yourself or others.

  ✔ To observe a reaction, look at the tube from the side. Never look down the tube.

✔ **Beakers and Flasks**

  ✔ Always support the container that is being heated on an iron ring above the burner. Use a wire gauze that has a ceramic center to disperse the flame and distribute heat evenly.

 **SAFE LABS**

Certain types of glassware are not meant to be heated. Volumetric glassware (for example, graduated cylinders, burettes, and pipets), funnels, jars, and watch glasses should never be heated. When these types of glassware are heated, they are subject to thermal stresses that will cause them to crack or shatter.

 DID YOU KNOW?

An easy rule to remember when considering heat dissipation in glassware is that rounded glassware will dissipate heat easier than glassware with sharper corners will. Therefore, a round-bottomed flask can handle higher thermal stresses than an Erlenmeyer flask or a beaker can. Another rule is that the thicker the walls of the glassware, the less able it is to tolerate thermal stresses.

CHAPTER 8

✔ Adjust gas flow to produce gradual heating of the beaker or flask; rapid heating will cause vigorous boiling and splashing.

✔ The flame should not touch the bottom of the container.

✔ **Crucibles**

✔ Clay triangles are used to support crucibles. Make sure the triangle you are using is the correct size to properly support the crucible you want to use. Do not use triangles that have broken or crumbling clay pipes.

✔ Always leave the lid on the crucible slightly open to permit vapors to escape. Position the lid so that the opening is not directed toward you or another person.

Are fumes or vapors of concern?

Carefully planned activities should not generate sufficient fumes or vapors to create problems. However, the danger that a student may use more chemical than the activity prescribes or that a container or gas line may leak always exist. If allowed to sufficiently concentrate, fumes or vapors may form an explosive mixture with air (or another substance) and create a thermal hazard. Some vapors may be heavier than air, so they collect along tabletops, in sinks, in trash cans, or along the floor. Stories of someone throwing a recently extinguished match into a sink or "empty" trash can and setting off an explosion are not uncommon. In addition, merely turning on the lights can cause an explosion if natural gas leaks into a closed room for a period of time. Listed below are some tips to avoid problems with fumes or vapors.

✔ Always check that gas valves have been completely closed at the end of the activity.

✔ Have students immediately report any odors of gas.

✔ If entering a room that smells of gas, do not let anyone else into the room until the room has been checked.

✔ Open windows to dissipate any gas that has accumulated in the room.

 SAFETY SUGGESTIONS

The possibility of a gas leak or the generation of fumes are good reasons for providing constant supervision of students during an experiment and for requiring students to report all accidents.

OTHER HAZARDS

What are radiation hazards?

Of all of the hazards described in this book, students (and the public) may think of **radiation hazards** as the most common and most dangerous hazards in the classroom. This concern is typically for ionizing radiation, which mainly results from radioactive decay. Often, people unreasonably fear any level of this type of radiation, even those levels that can be considered safe. Unfortunately, hazards from other forms of radiation, such as lasers, microwaves, and visible light, are frequently unrecognized. This chapter will discuss all types of the radiation hazards but will emphasize the types of radiation that are often ignored—nonionizing radiation hazards.

 **DEFINITIONS**

radiation hazard
any device or substance that produces nonionizing or ionizing radiation

What are nonionizing radiation hazards?

Nonionizing radiation is any form of electromagnetic radiation that has a wavelength greater than or equal to 100 nm. This part of the electromagnetic spectrum includes ultraviolet waves, visible waves, infrared waves, microwaves, and radio waves. Photons in this energy range are not energetic enough to remove electrons from atoms; therefore, they are nonionizing radiation. These waves can, however, create harmful effects, so they are hazards.

What are microwaves?

Microwaves are a portion of the electromagnetic spectrum. The frequencies of microwaves can range from 10 MHz to 100 GHz. Microwaves are usually characterized by their frequency range because their wavelengths depend on the media through which they pass. Microwaves have shorter wavelengths in biological media than in gaseous media such as air. In addition, they are reflected from metallic surfaces.

What are some sources of microwaves?

Microwave ovens are, of course, sources of microwaves. The only other sources of microwave radiation in your classroom should be from demonstration apparatus. Typically, most types of demonstration apparatus are relatively harmless if no one tries to alter them, because they have low power.

What harmful effects does microwave radiation produce?

Microwave radiation can be harmful, and these waves can affect various organs and tissues differently. The following is a list of the effects which microwave radiation can produce.

❏ Surgical implants that contain metal can absorb electromagnetic energy. This absorption can create electrical currents that can damage the implants. The absorption of microwave energy may also generate heat, which may cause pain or injury to surrounding tissue. An example of implants that are affected by microwave radiation is a pacemaker.

❑ Microwave radiation can cause damage to organs or systems by either disrupting their functions or changing their structure. Studies have suggested that chronic low-level exposure to microwaves lowers blood pressure and changes the heart rate or rhythm. Microwaves that have high power densities can cause genetic damage, such as chromosomal aberrations and mutations. These biological effects are caused by the heat generated as cells absorb microwave energy.

❑ Microwave exposure at high power in small areas ($>10 \, \text{mW/cm}^2$) produces body heating, which is typically controlled by thermoregulatory mechanisms, such as sweating or blood flow. Areas that have poor blood flow (such as the eyes and testes) are therefore more susceptible to injury by microwaves.

❑ Microwaves can cause damage to an eye by heating it. Serious injuries include lens opacities, cataracts, corneal changes, and retinal lesions. Injuries that are less serious and that will not permanently damage the eye are irritation and inflammation of the conjunctiva, cornea, and iris. The threshold for injuries from a long ($>30 \, \text{min}$) exposure to microwaves depends on the frequency of the radiation, as shown in the table below.

Eye Injuries After One Hour of Exposure

Frequency	Power Density	Type of Eye Injury
$<2 \, \text{GHz}$	all values	minor only
$2–10 \, \text{GHz}$	$30 \, \text{mW/cm}^2$	some corneal damage
$>10 \, \text{GHz}$	$100 \, \text{mW/cm}^2$	corneal opacities and cataracts

What is the acceptable limit for microwave exposure?

The accepted limit for continuous, daily exposure to microwaves is $10 \, \text{mW/cm}^2$. No one in your classroom should ever be exposed to microwaves over $100 \, \text{mW/cm}^2$. Power-density exposure is only one of several factors that can affect the damage caused by microwaves. The other factors are

❑ frequency and wavelength of microwaves

❑ duration of exposure to microwaves

❑ part of the body (tissues/organs) exposed to the microwaves

❑ orientation of the person to the microwave source

❑ environmental conditions, such as temperature and drafts

❑ effects from reflected microwave energy

❏ cycling of the microwave source (magnetron) or number of active periods during exposure

How can I avoid accidents caused by microwave sources?

To avoid accidents caused by microwave sources, follow the tips below.

✔ Follow manufacturers' instructions when you use microwave sources.

✔ Do not alter the microwave source in any way.

✔ Never defeat the safety interlocks of a microwave source.

✔ Check the microwave source for leaks before you use the apparatus. Inexpensive microwave detectors are available from instrument or safety-equipment sellers.

✔ Check the condition of the microwave source.

✔ Place shields between the demonstration and your students.

✔ Keep students away from apparatus or ovens.

✔ Never place metal objects in microwave ovens.

✔ Place a heat sink, such as a container of water, inside your microwave oven.

✔ Do not wear watches, rings, or jewelry near high-frequency microwave fields.

✔ Direct microwave beams away from you and your students.

✔ Be aware of any reflected microwave beams.

 SAFETY INFORMATION

Guidelines for protection from microwave energy are provided in the American National Standard "Safety Levels with Respect to Human Exposure to Radio Frequency Electromagnetic Fields, 300 kHz to 100 GHz, ANSI C95.1."

What do I need to know about other forms of radiation?

The following table contains information about ultraviolet, visible, and infrared light. Remember that any form of light (radiation) can be dangerous, regardless of its frequency.

Information about Ultraviolet, Visible, and Infrared Light

Designation	Wavelength	Comments
UV-C (far)	<280 nm	"Germicidal" region; can disinfect or clean
UV-B (mid)	315–280 nm	"Erythemal" region; is biologically active
UV-A (near)	400–315 nm	"Black-light" region; induces fluorescence
VIS	400–750 nm	"White" light; includes all visible light
IR-A (near)	750–1400 nm	type of IR that penetrates living tissue the deepest

CHAPTER 9

| IR-B | 1.4–3 μm | heavily absorbed by water; slightly penetrates living tissue |
| IR-C (far) | 3 μm–1 mm | absorbs superficially; doesn't penetrate eye or skin |

What are some sources of these types of radiation?

Light always surrounds us, frequently from obvious sources of light such as the fluorescent lights in your classroom. Some of the other sources may not be as obvious. For example, ultraviolet sources include

- ❏ arc lamps
- ❏ spectrograph sources
- ❏ germicidal lamps
- ❏ mercury vapor and xenon lamps
- ❏ some photocopiers
- ❏ the sun

Very hot solid substances may produce some ultraviolet radiation; however, most of these substances emit infrared radiation. Infrared radiation is also produced by infrared lasers and lamps, the sun, electric arcs used for illumination, and sources that are so hot that they are incandescent.

 DID YOU KNOW?

Low-pressure illumination arcs produce spectra that have discrete lines, but high-pressure illumination arcs produce spectra that are fairly continuous. Incandescent sources emit radiation continuously over a broad spectrum.

What injuries do these types of radiation cause?

All types of radiation can damage living tissue, and the more energetic the radiation is, the more damaging the radiation is. Read the list below for the types of injuries ultraviolet, visible, and infrared radiation can cause.

Ultraviolet radiation (This type of radiation can be especially hazardous because it cannot be seen or initially felt.)

- ❏ Ultraviolet radiation may cause changes in proteins and DNA.
- ❏ Ultraviolet radiation immediately affects the skin by darkening the skin's pigment, by causing suntan and sunburn (primarily at wavelengths >300 nm), and by creating cell-growth changes (ultraviolet radiation initially stops cell growth and then promotes rapid cell-growth rates). Long-term damages include skin aging and skin cancer.
- ❏ The eye can completely absorb ultraviolet radiation; absorption occurs primarily in the cornea, sclera, and conjunctiva.

If the wavelength or the radiation is greater than 300 nm, the lens and tissues of the eye's interior may be exposed. "Welder's flash," or photokeratitis, is a common result of a UV-radiation hazard. Tissue damage depends on the length of exposure. Injuries and conditions that are caused by ultraviolet-radiation exposure include excessive buildup of blood (hyperemia), light sensitivity (photophobia), and eyelid spasms (blepharospasm).

 DID YOU KNOW?

The most common phototoxic effect is sunburn. This damage can be intensified for people who take photosensitive drugs (certain antibiotics and antibacterials, laxatives, tranquilizers, or antihistamines). People taking these medications risk sunburn from the ultraviolet emissions of fluorescent lamps.

Visible and infrared radiation

❑ Photochemical effects on living tissue are significant only at short wavelengths (>500 nm). Light that has wavelengths ranging from 400 nm to 500 nm causes photochemical injuries to the retina after only several seconds of exposure. This damage is frequently caused by viewing a solar eclipse.

❑ Long-term exposures of IR-A of approximately 100 mW/cm^2 to the eye may produce cataracts. Short-term exposures of IR-A at 4 W/cm^2 to the eye may also produce cataracts.

❑ Thermal injuries are the major injuries caused by longer visible light and infrared wavelengths. (However, some of these wavelengths tend to be focused on and absorbed by the retina and choroid of the eye, so you should not allow anyone to stare at light sources.) These thermal effects are dependent on the irradiance (W/cm^2) and are not very dependent on wavelength. Short-pulse sources, such as flash lamps, can cause thermal injuries. Because of the extreme brightness of short-pulse sources, blood circulation and conduction cannot dissipate the heat produced by these sources quickly enough.

How can I avoid accidents during the use of light sources?

To avoid accidents using these sources, follow the tips below.

✔ "Shortwave" (UV-B and UV-C) and "longwave" (UV-A) mode instruments should be labeled.

✔ Provide protection from these light sources by using opaque or translucent screens and curtains. These shields will attenuate ultraviolet radiation and filter or diffuse light to a safer level.

✔ Remind students that housings for optical sources may become hot after use, so students should careful while touching these sources.

✔ Never view the sun directly; always project the image of the sun on a screen or wall. Use

 SAFETY INFORMATION

"Black-light" lamps are not usually considered hazardous. However, if the lamp envelope insufficiently filters the ultraviolet radiation or if the user is photosensitive, skin reactions, conjunctivitis, or photokeratitis can occur.

CHAPTER 9

welder's glass (carefully), if available, or mount a solar filter on a telescope.

✔ Tell students of the hazards of light, and instruct students on how to use light sources.

✔ Use and have your students use protective eyewear and apparel.

Just what is a laser?

The term *laser* is an acronym for "light amplification by stimulated emission of radiation." Lasers are devices that produce and amplify light. Laser light can be characterized by properties that are very desirable but almost impossible to obtain by any other devices. In particular, laser light is almost monochromatic and has low beam divergence. Lasers consist of optical cavities, appropriate lasing mediums (gases, solids, or liquids can be used), and pumping or exciter systems. In addition, lasers are commonly designated by the type of material that causes the production of laser light. The four classifications of lasers are solid state, gas, dye (liquid), and semiconductor.

Types of lasers

Several types of lasers are available. A laser is named according to the medium in which the lasing takes place. Lasers can produce either continuous light or pulsed light. These first two types are often operated in classrooms.

❏ **Helium Neon Laser**
One of the most common and widely used types of lasers is the helium neon (HeNe) laser. Although the first successful operation of this type of laser was at an infrared wavelength of 1.15 μm, the HeNe laser is most well known for producing red 633 nm light. Some HeNe lasers today also can emit light at other wavelengths (such as 612 nm, 594 nm, and 543 nm). The power from a HeNe laser ranges from a fraction of a milliwatt to about 75 mW.

❏ **Semiconductor Diode Lasers**
The semiconductor or diode-injection laser is a type of solid state laser. Semiconductor diode lasers are used only to produce light in the near infrared spectral region. However, recently made semiconductor diode lasers can produce visible light.

Note that the following laser types are too powerful for instructional activities and introduce unnecessary dangers when operated in classroom settings.

❏ **Argon, Krypton, or Xenon Ion Laser**
These ion lasers use argon, krypton, xenon, and neon gases to provide sources for over 35 different laser frequencies, which range from the near ultraviolet (neon at 322 nm) to the near infrared (krypton at 799 nm). It is possible to mix these gases to produce either a single frequency of light or a simultaneous emission of light at 10 different wavelengths. These lasers can produce up to 20 W of power—well beyond the needs of instructional activities.

❏ **Carbon Dioxide Laser**
The carbon dioxide laser is the most efficient and most powerful continuous laser. The power output of these lasers have been reported above 30 kW at the far infrared wavelength of 10.6 μm. Again, this type of laser should not used in instructional activities.

❏ **Nd:YAG Laser Systems**
This laser source is one of the most widely used, and yields moderate to high power using a neodymium-doped Yttrium Aluminum Garnet (YAG) crystal. These lasers are often called *Nd:YAG lasers* and are capable of continuous outputs of approximately 1000 W and have a wavelength of 1.06 μm.

> ☑ **DID YOU KNOW?**
>
> Nd:YAG lasers are solid-state lasers. Solid-state lasers are a unique milestone in laser development. The first operational solid-state laser medium was a crystal of pink ruby (a sapphire crystal doped with chromium). Now, the term *solid state laser* is usually used to describe a laser whose active medium is a crystal doped with an impurity ion. Solid-state lasers are rugged, simple to maintain, and capable of generating high power. Solid-state lasers usually produce a large number of separated power bursts rather than a continuous beam.

❏ **Excimer Lasers**
Excimer (abbreviation for the term *excited dimer*) lasers operate using reactive gases, such as chlorine and fluorine, and inert gases, such as argon, krypton, or xenon. The various gas combinations, when electrically excited, produce a short-lived molecule (called a *dimer*). The energy-level configuration of this molecule causes the generation of laser light that has a specific wavelength. These laser systems have a average power range of 50W to 100 W.

❏ **Dye Lasers**
Dye lasers were the first true tunable lasers. Using different organic dyes, dye lasers are capable of producing light in the range of ultraviolet to near infrared. Most dye lasers are operated so that they produce visible light that has tunable emissions that are red, yellow, green, or blue.

CHAPTER 9

What are the classifications of lasers?

By law, all lasers that are commercially available are classified according to four categories. This classification is used to identify the hazards associated with the levels of radiation that the lasers produce. These categories of lasers should be indicated through the use of labels, signs, and instruction.

These categories are based on the ability of a laser beam to cause biological damage to eye tissue or skin tissue and help define appropriate control measures. In the Federal Laser Product Performance Standard (FLPPS), the classes are established relative to the Accessible Emission Limits (AEL), which is defined in the American National Standards Institute Z-136 standard.

❏ **Class I**

A laser that is incapable of emitting laser radiation at known hazardous power levels (typically a continuous wave [CW] of 0.4 μW at visible wavelengths) is a Class I laser. Class I laser products are generally exempt from radiation hazard controls during operation and maintenance (but not necessarily during service). Note that a Class I laser system may actually contain a laser that could be classified differently. Such systems are designated Class I because the laser is imbedded in the system and is difficult to access separately.

❏ **Class IIA**

This class is a special designation for lasers and applies only to lasers that are "not intended for viewing," such as a supermarket laser scanner. The maximum power limit of Class IIA is 0.4 mW. The emission from a Class IIA laser is defined such that the emission does not exceed the Class I limit for an emission that has a duration of 1000 s.

❏ **Class II**

Lasers that emit visible light and have powers ranging from 0.4 μW to 1 mW are Class II lasers. It is believed that the human aversion reaction to the bright light will protect a person from lengthy exposures to such lasers, so only limited controls and precautions are specified for them.

❏ **Class IIIA**

Lasers that produce 1 mW to 5 mW of continuous wave power are Class IIIA lasers. These lasers are hazardous only for intrabeam viewing. Some limited controls and precautions for these lasers are usually recommended.

❏ **Class IIIB**

Class IIIB lasers are lasers that produce 5 mW to 500 mW of continuous wave power or 10 J/cm^2 of pulsed power. In general, Class IIIB lasers are not fire hazards and rarely produce a hazardous diffuse reflection. Specific controls and precautions are recommended when these lasers are in use. They are not appropriate for classroom use or instructional activities.

❑ **Class IV**
High-power Class IV lasers (continuous wave power: 500 mW; pulsed power: 10 J/cm^2) are hazardous to eyes because the light from these lasers can be absorbed by eyes whether the light is directly or diffusely scattered. These lasers are also potential fire hazards and are hazardous to skin and other living tissues. Significant controls and precautions are required for the use of Class IV lasers. These lasers should never be used in a classroom.

Laser manufacturers are required by law to provide laser classification labels. The class of the laser will be specified only on the lower left-hand corner of the manufacturer's label. The label must contain the laser "sunburst" symbol and the word "CAUTION" (for Class II and some Class IIIA lasers) or "DANGER" (for some Class IIIA and all Class IIIB and Class IV lasers). This label will also have the type of laser (for example, HeNe, Argon, or CO_2) and the power or energy output (for example, 1 mW CW/MAX or 100 mJ pulsed).

Although the FLPPS requires no classification labels for Class I lasers, it does require detailed compliance with numerous other performance requirements (for example, protective housing, other labels, and interlocking).

What hazards are associated with lasers?

Hazards associated with the low-power lasers commonly used in instructional activities are minimal. Because more powerful lasers may become a part of instructional activities, you should be aware of the potential hazards of all lasers.

A laser is an almost ideal point source of intense light. Most lasers have sufficient power to produce retinal intensities that are theoretically orders of magnitude greater than those produced by conventional light sources and even the sun.

Thermal energy is the most common cause of laser-induced tissue damage. Tissue proteins are denatured due to the temperature rise following absorption of laser energy. Burns are generally associated with lasers operating at exposure times greater than 10 μs and in the wavelength region from the near ultraviolet to the far infrared. Tissue damage may also be caused by thermally induced acoustic waves following submicrosecond exposures. For pulsed or scanning lasers, the major mechanism involved in laser-induced biological damage is also a thermal process, in which each pulse adds more thermal energy. Thermal effects of laser exposure depend upon the following factors.

❑ the absorption and scattering coefficients of the tissues at the laser wavelength

❑ irradiance or radiant exposure potential of the laser beam (output power)

❑ duration of the exposure

❑ pulse repetition characteristics, where applicable

❑ extent of the local vascular flow

❑ size of the irradiated area

Photochemical and skin reactions have been demonstrated for certain wavelength ranges or exposure times. Exposure in the UV-B range does the most damage to the skin. In addition to thermal injury caused by ultraviolet energy, radiation carcinogenesis from UV-B either directly on DNA or from the effects of potentially carcinogenic intracellular viruses is a possibility. Exposure in the shorter UV-C and the longer UV-A ranges seems less harmful to human skin. The shorter wavelengths are absorbed in the outer dead layers of the epidermis (stratum corneum) and the longer wavelengths have an initial pigment-darkening effect, which is followed by erythema if the skin is exposed to excessive levels of UV-A ranges.

The hazards associated with skin exposure are less hazardous than eye hazards; however, you must not forget that some laser beams may be effective some distance from their intended point of use.

How can I prevent accidents when lasers are used?

Accident data about laser usage have shown that Class I, Class II, Class IIA, and Class IIIA lasers do not normally constitute a radiation hazard unless illogically used. Some standard practices apply regardless of the type of laser or power output.

✔ Never look directly at the laser beam or at its specular reflection.

✔ Never point the laser at anything other than what is required by the activity.

✔ When aligning the laser or system components, always work above the plane of the beam.

✔ Never operate a laser with the cover removed (electrical hazard).

✔ Shield the beam so it cannot accidentally be aimed or reflected out of the door or windows or into neighboring work stations.

✔ Close the beam shutter during pauses in the activity.

✔ Use goggles and other protective equipment, including skin protection.

Again, only Class I, II, or IIIA lasers should be used in instructional activities. Class IIIB and IV lasers require procedures and controls well beyond what you or any teacher should want to handle. Use of lasers in these more-hazardous classes requires a written Standard Operating Procedure, the appointment of a Laser Safety Officer, and the purchase of suitable protective equipment for the system as well as for students and visitors.

What are ionizing radiation hazards?

Ionizing radiation hazards include substances that are radioactive and equipment that produces or contains such substances. Radioactivity is a property of certain unstable nuclides and results from a process in which unstable nuclides reach a more stable nuclear state. When emissions from radioactive atoms interact with other atoms, particles in nonradioactive atoms can be ejected. For this reason, radioactivity is described as ionizing radiation.

 SAFETY SUGGESTIONS

Laboratory equipment that produces ionizing radiation must be used very carefully. In addition, the concept of radioactivity and the appropriate precautions for handling radioactive substances and devices must be clearly and completely explained to students and other teachers. People often have an unreasonable fear of any type or amount of radiation and do not know that certain levels of radiation can be safe when protection and care are used.

What is radioactive decay?

Radioactive decay is a property of the nuclei of atoms. The process of radioactive decay is not affected by temperature, pressure, magnetic and electric fields, or chemical bonding. Radioactive decay can occur by several processes, which are described below.

❏ **Alpha Emission**
Alpha emission occurs when a nucleus decays into a daughter nucleus and an alpha particle. The ejected alpha particle has the same mass and charge as a helium-4 nucleus. Kinetic energies of alpha particles typically range from 1.8 MeV to 8 MeV, which corresponds to speeds ranging from 9×10^6 m/s to 2×10^7 m/s.

❏ **Beta Emission**
Beta emission occurs when a neutron of a nucleus converts into a proton, and an electron, an antineutrino, and energy are released. The ejected electron is called a beta particle.

CHAPTER 9

Beta-particle energies range from 0.1 to 2.5 MeV, which corresponds to speeds from 3×10^7 m/s to 3×10^8 m/s.

❑ **Positron Emission**

Positron emission typically occurs only in particle accelerators. During positron emission, a proton of a nucleus changes into a neutron, and a positron and a neutrino are ejected from the nucleus. The positron is very short-lived because it interacts immediately with an electron. This interaction results in the annihilation of the electron and the positron and in the production of two photons. Positron kinetic energies range from 0.3 MeV to 2.8 MeV, which corresponds to speeds from 2×10^8 m/s to 3×10^8 m/s.

 **DID YOU KNOW?**

Beta emission, positron emission, and electron capture are all considered types of beta decay.

❑ **Electron Capture**

Electron capture occurs primarily in particle accelerators and is a competitive process to positron emission. During electron capture, an electron from an atom is captured by that atom's nucleus, which converts a proton into a neutron and ejects a neutrino. X rays are generated when other electrons of the atom rearrange to fill the vacancy made by the captured electron.

❑ **Gamma Emission and Internal Conversion**

If a nucleus is excited to an energy greater than the energy of its ground state, the nucleus may emit a photon (gamma ray). This process is called *gamma emission*. The excess energy of the excited nucleus may also be transferred to an electron that is in the atom. This electron is then ejected from the atom and the other electrons rearrange to fill the void. X rays are emitted during this "internal conversion" process.

What are some sources of radiation?

Sources of exposure to ionizing radiation can be natural or artificially produced. Natural sources include cosmic, terrestrial, and internal sources. The majority of natural radiation exposure is caused by the inhalation of nuclides made during radon decay. Artificially produced radiation comes from medical and dental X rays, consumer products, and industrial, military, and research activities.

Many of the radiation sources intended for educational use have such low activities that these sources present minimal health hazards. If a source must be licensed, then that source is dangerous enough that defined precautions are necessary. Even if a source does not have to be licensed, all radioactive materials should be handled with care and in a professional manner.

Many radioactive sources can be purchased for instructional use. They are usually sealed and their activities are very low, so licenses are not required to use them. In addition, some radioactive equipment used for instruction include containers of parent sources (cesium and barium). These sources are eluted by weak acid solutions to produce the liquid daughters. Gas discharge tubes that produce X rays and X-ray systems for instructional use are also radioactive sources.

What are the units used in measurements of radioactive material?

The following units are used for measurements of radioactive material and express activity, exposure, and dose of radioactive material.

❏ **Curie and Becquerel (SI)**
The curie (C) and the becquerel (Bq) are the basic units of radioactive decay. They measure the rate at which a radioactive nucleus disintegrates. The curie was chosen to approximate the decay rate of 1 g of radium-226.
Activity: 1 curie, $C = 3.7 \times 10^{10}$ becquerel
$Bq = 3.7 \times 10^{10}$ decay events per second

❏ **Roentgens and Coulombs per Kilogram (SI)**
Exposure to ionizing radiation is given in roentgens (R) or in coulombs per kilogram. These units measure exposure in terms of the amount of charge produced by ionizing radiation. They are the basic units for measuring gamma or X-ray radiation. A roentgen is a large quantity of radiation; the more common unit is the milliroentgen (mR).
Exposure: 1 roentgen = the production of ions carrying a charge of 2.58×10^{-4} coulomb per kg of air

❏ **Rad and Gray (SI)**
Rad and gray (Gy) are units that describe any material's energy absorption, which occurs at a point and is caused by any ionizing radiation. If the material is living tissue, these units are dose units. If the material is air, these units are exposure units. The quantities represented by these units correspond to observable biological effects.
Absorbed Dose: 1 rad = 0.01 gray
Gy = 0.01 J energy/ kg material

❏ **Rem and Sievert (SI)**
The rem and the sievert (Sv) are units of dose equivalent. These units express the biological effect of the absorbed dose in humans. In most cases, dose equivalent is proportional to the product of the absorbed dose in rad (or gray) and a factor

that accounts for the effects of that type of radiation on an organism.

Dose Equivalent: 1 rem = 0.01 sievert

Sv = damage to human body produced by 1 R

How does radiation damage living tissue?

Radiation can damage cells in many ways. Cells in the body are damaged primarily through alterations of DNA. However, some cells can be killed directly by radiation damage. Cells that are dividing and tissue that form blood cells are more susceptible to radiation damage than other cells and tissue are. Cells damaged by radiation may contribute to the development of various diseases even if the cells are not killed. Even if a cell is not extensively damaged by radiation, it probably will not be able to repair itself effectively.

Exposures to radiation may be acute (short-term exposure and high dose of radiation) or chronic (long-term exposure and low dose of radiation). Radiation exposure can also be external or internal. External exposure is due to a source located outside the body, while internal exposure is due to a source placed inside the body. Radioactive materials can be introduced internally by inhalation, ingestion, absorption, or injection. Gamma and X rays can be very dangerous to people who have been exposed to them in any way, because these types of radiation have large energies and can penetrate deep into skin and tissue. However, alpha particles are not very dangerous to people exposed externally to them because they have small energies and cannot penetrate the skin. Alpha particles that are inhaled, ingested, or injected can be very dangerous.

 **DID YOU KNOW?**

Young people have more rapidly dividing cells than adults, and these cells are most susceptible to radiation damage. This is why young people are often more affected by radiation doses than adults are.

What are the dose limits for radiation exposure?

Recommended exposure limits vary slightly between agencies. The Nuclear Regulatory Commission (in 10CFR Part 20.101) limits exposure to the general population to 1.0 mSv (0.1 rem). The National Council on Radiation Protection and Measurements also have recommendations for education and training dose limits. The exposure limits are 1 mSv (0.1 rem) annually to prevent stochastic (random) effects, 15 mSv (1.5 rem) to the eye lens and 5 mSv (0.5 rem) to any square centimeter area of skin or to the hands and feet to prevent nonstochastic effects.

How can I avoid accidents while using sources of ionizing radiation?

You can do many things to avoid accidents while using ionizing radiation. One method is to avoid using ionizing radiation. For example, if you want to demonstrate a radioactive decay process, you can use water, marbles, candy, or pennies to model exponential growth. If you do choose to use radioactive sources, remember that you must follow government guidelines, which could include writing a radiation control program or appointing a radiation safety officer. Listed below are some tips to avoid accidents while using ionizing radiation.

General

✔ Know federal, state, and local regulations regarding the purchase, use, storage, and disposal of radioactive material.

✔ Avoid having students handle radioactive sources.

✔ Tell students about the radioactive sources that they are observing or using and about any precautions that the students must take.

✔ Post signs that warn students about the hazards of the radioactive sources in your classroom.

✔ Do not allow anyone to eat or drink while radioactive sources are in your classroom.

✔ Purchase only quantities of these radioactive substances that do not require licenses.

✔ Purchase the least amount of a radioactive substance that you need for an experiment.

✔ Inquire about handling, usage, and disposal requirements before ordering a particular radioactive material.

✔ Store radioactive materials in a specially designated area in which appropriate containers and shielding are accessible. Promptly return materials to storage after use.

✔ Take special precautions to prevent unauthorized personnel from removing radioactive materials from your storage area.

✔ Always minimize the exposure of you or your students to a radioactive source. Frequent or prolonged contact with a source can result in significant localized radiation exposure.

✔ Wear gloves, goggles, and an apron when working with radioactive sources.

Sealed Radioactive Sources

✔ Handle sealed sources carefully to avoid breaking the seals.

✔ Use tongs or forceps to handle sealed sources.

✔ Dispose of all sources through your local radiation safety officer or chemical waste company.

Unsealed Radioactive Sources

✔ Prepare liquid samples in a designated preparation area. Use a tray that has a lip and is lined with paper towels to contain any spills.

✔ Wear gloves, goggles, and an apron when working with liquid sources, but do not then wear these protective devices outside the room in which you worked with the radioactive sources.

✔ Make sure that sources do not contact skin, mouth, or open sores or cuts.

✔ Wash hands and forearms with soap and water after handling radioactive materials.

✔ Do not pipette the liquid with your mouth. (This rule applies to all solution, especially radioactive solutions.)

✔ Place planchettes (or another source container) in a large beaker of water to allow the sample to decay before drain disposal. Wash source containers after use.

✔ Dispose of radioactive materials in the proper manner. Also dispose of or clean contaminated materials such as paper towels and glassware in the proper manner.

Devices That Produce Radiation

✔ Do not excite Crookes' tubes with variable spark gap induction coils.

✔ Do not use discharge tubes made of hard glass. Soft glass tubes weaken X rays, which makes the X rays slightly less dangerous.

✔ Never operate tubes that produce X rays with a power source whose output is not precisely known, cannot be precisely controlled, or drifts significantly. Beware of "home-built" power supplies.

✔ Always orient equipment to minimize the exposure of you or your students to radiation.

✔ Never operate instructional X-ray systems without protective shields or covers in place.

✔ Never try to defeat interlocks or other safety devices.

✔ Always follow manufacturers' maintenance procedures. Promptly report any problems to the manufacturers.

 SAFE LABS

The following lab is an alternative method to show radioactive decay.
MATERIALS
pennies and plastic cups
PROCEDURE
1. Count the pennies your teacher has given you and record this number as "start."
2. Place the pennies in a plastic cup. Cover the cup with one hand, and gently shake it for several seconds.
3. Pour the pennies on your desk or laboratory table. Remove all the pennies that are heads up. Count the remaining pennies, and record this number and the number of times you have performed step 2.
4. Repeat steps 2 and 3 until you have no pennies to place in your cup.
5. Plot your data on graph paper. Label the x-axis "Number of times step 2 was performed," and label the y-axis "Number of pennies."

What labels and signs should I use?

The following table lists the minimum amount of radioactive material that a sample can have before the manufacturer must label the sample's container as radioactive. In addition, the room or area in which radioactive materials or equipment are stored should have a sign that warns people of their presence. An example of an appropriate sign is "CAUTION (or DANGER)—RADIOACTIVE MATERIAL(S)."

Quantities of Some Common Radioisotopes That Require Labeling

Material	mCi
Barium-133	10
Cesium-137	10
Cobalt-60	1
Polonium-210	0.1
Strontium-90	1

SAFETY INFORMATION

The quantities of some common radioisotopes that require labeling is taken from the Nuclear Regulatory Commission, 10CFR 20, Appendix C.

Posting requirements for radiation exposures due to apparatus or sources are given in the following table. According to OSHA 29CFR 1910.96, you do not have to post the presence of sealed sources if the surface of the radioactive material 12 in. from the surface of the source container or housing is less than or equal to 5 mrem/h.

Signs for Various Radiation Levels

Potential Dose	Sign
>0.005 rem/h and ≤0.1 rem/h	CAUTION: RADIATION AREA
>0.1 rem/h and ≤500 rem/h	CAUTION (or DANGER): HIGH RADIATION AREA
Any X-ray machine	CAUTION: HIGH-INTENSITY X RAYS

What type of shields should I use with sources of ionizing radiation?

Shields can minimize radiation exposure and should be used when possible. The activity of the radioactive source and the type and energy of the radiation determine the type and thickness of the shield. Tips for when to use shields and what types of shields to use are listed below.

✔ Alpha sources do not require shields because the dead outer layer of skin absorbs them.

CHAPTER 9

✔ Beta sources generate **bremsstrahlung,** so shielding material must be made of elements that have low atomic numbers. Lucite and Plexiglas are particularly good choices for shields. In addition, shields that are made of the proper materials should be 1 cm thick to stop beta particles from all common beta emitters used as radioisotopes.

✔ Lead is the most common type of shielding for gamma and X-ray sources. A lead brick that is 5 cm thick will reduce the gamma intensity from most common emitters by a factor of 10.

✔ A radioactive source emits radioactive material in all directions, so shield the entire source or device.

✔ The necessary thickness of shielding for X rays depends on the voltage of the tube. For example, a tube with a 50 kV accelerating potential would require a lead shield that is 0.06 mm thick and a tube with a 300 kV accelerating potential would require a lead shield that is 1.5 mm thick.

✔ Aluminum sheets that are about 0.5 mm to 3 mm thick can be used as shields from "soft" X rays, depending on the accelerating potential of the X rays.

 DEFINITIONS

bremsstrahlung
the electromagnetic radiation released by a high-energy particle, such as an electron, when it is suddenly accelerated or retarded by an electric field or another charged particle, such as an atomic nucleus

LEGAL ISSUES

Why should I learn about legal issues?

School administrators are typically the only personnel to receive training in classroom liability issues, yet teachers have the most responsibility for the safety of their students. Although administrators are certainly targets for lawsuits, teachers can also be sued. In addition, teachers are in the best position to prevent accidents in the classroom and to prevent any resulting lawsuits. This chapter introduces some basic ideas about the legal duties of a teacher and provides a basic discussion of negligence. (Students and administrators also have responsibilities for safety, but their responsibilities are beyond the scope of this chapter.)

Fear of lawsuits should not be the dominant factor in determining how to organize your class. You should always be concerned about the safety of everyone in your classroom, regardless of the legal issues. But as you limit your liability, you will also create a safer classroom.

 **SAFETY SUGGESTIONS**

Federal, state, and local legislation and regulations establish teachers' liability and responsibility for students' safety. These laws and regulations are outside the scope of this book, but you should become familiar with the requirements that apply to you.

How am I liable?

You may be held liable for an accident if you are negligent in performing a duty and that negligence contributes to an accident. Imprudent or negligent acts can take many forms. A few examples are

- ❑ teaching a course that you are improperly trained to teach
- ❑ failing to warn students clearly about hazards in the classroom or in an experiment
- ❑ using equipment that you know is broken
- ❑ being absent from or inattentive in your classroom while an accident occurs
- ❑ making students perform a hazardous activity
- ❑ failing to provide proper or adequate safety equipment

What are my responsibilities as a teacher?

You have three duties as a teacher that require your attention to avoid liability for an accident: instruction, supervision, and maintenance. A description of each responsibility is listed below.

 SAFETY INFORMATION

These three duties are taken from *Better Science Through Safety*, by Jack Gerlovich and Gary Downs. See the appendix for more information.

- ❑ **Instruction** In the context of this chapter, instruction means providing appropriate and pertinent information to your students so that they may safely complete an activity. Instruction can take a variety of forms:

❑ explanations and warnings (written and verbal) about apparatus, materials (for example, chemicals), and procedures

❑ step-by-step instructions (written and verbal) for an experiment or for using equipment

❑ warnings (written and verbal) about the hazards related to operating equipment or performing experiments

❑ signs warning students of a particular hazard

❑ activities designed to teach students how to handle certain hazards

Instruction can appear in laboratory manuals, handouts, overheads, and computer software. Both written and verbal methods should be used because repetition of instructions ensures that students have been informed. From a legal point of view, using written explanations and warnings will provide you with evidence that you have fulfilled your duty of instruction if an accident occurs in your classroom.

You should also ensure that students understand your instructions. You can test your students' understanding by

✔ questioning your students directly

✔ giving safety-related quizzes, tests, and worksheets

✔ having your students prepare papers and laboratory reports regarding safety

Written assessments also provide you with important documentary evidence that you have fulfilled your duty of instruction.

❑ **Supervision** Your duty of supervision is straightforward—you must be present and attentive when students are in your classroom. If an accident occurs, your presence in the classroom will be of less benefit if you are simply grading homework or talking with a colleague. Fulfilling the duty of supervision also means more than merely being attentive to your students. The degree of supervision must be tailored to the specific activity and the needs of the students who are engaging in the activity. Consider the following list as you determine the appropriate degree of supervision for a given situation.

❑ Activities involving potentially hazardous materials or procedures require a higher degree of supervision than activities with less potential for hazards.

SAFETY SUGGESTIONS

Discuss hazards and safety precautions with your students before and during demonstrations even if your students are not directly involved in the activity. This discussion helps students become aware of hazards and safety. More important, inquisitive students often try to duplicate demonstrations on their own, and the results are sometimes unfortunate. Explaining the hazards and safety precautions for a demonstration may deter students from trying an unsupervised demonstration.

❑ Chemistry and biology activities generally require a higher degree of supervision than physics or astronomy activities do.

❑ Younger or immature students require a higher degree of supervision than older or more mature students do.

❑ Students with disabilities may require more supervision than students without disabilities do.

❑ Students who are conducting an outdoor activity or who are on a field trip require more supervision than students in the classroom do.

❑ **Maintenance** At first glance, you may wonder what maintenance has to do with teaching. Maintenance primarily refers to the upkeep of instructional apparatus in your classroom. You must ensure that all apparatus are in safe condition. This requirement includes demonstration apparatus that you use as a teacher as well as apparatus that your students use.

The facilities must also be well maintained. If you find an unsafe condition, such as a leaking sink, burned-out lamps, or a broken lock on a storage cabinet, you should report the condition immediately so that the problem is addressed. You must also ensure that your students are not exposed to an unsafe condition.

What can happen if I fail in my responsibilities?

In general, if a legal duty exists, any conduct below the prevailing standard of care is negligent. Negligence has several definitions, which include the following:

❑ careless conduct

❑ failure to use the degree of care required by circumstances at the time of the act

❑ failure to use the care that an ordinary, prudent person would use under the same or similar circumstances to avoid causing injury to another or to protect another from injury

❑ conduct in spite of recognizable danger or injury

❑ conduct that incurs an unreasonable risk of causing damage

Note that all of these ways to understand negligence deal with conduct, not your state of mind or your intentions. A hope that no student would be injured is not a good defense if you were to have to defend yourself in court. Only identifiable actions you took to prevent an injury can show that you were not negligent. Although by definition an accident is unavoidable and does not constitute negligence, an accident can be caused by a negligent act. So, if an accident occurs, you can be sued for negligence.

A suit that involves negligence can be settled in a court of law. Courts do know that children tend to be accident prone, but you should not depend on this knowledge as your defense. The best way to handle this type of suit is to prevent the suit from being filed in the first place by regularly taking actions to prevent injury to students.

What is a tort?

Cases of negligence are classified as torts. A **tort** is committed when an act you perform or fail to perform violates someone's rights. The teacher-student relationship is such that the teacher is required to act to prevent injury to the student if a potential and recognized danger exists. To do otherwise is to violate the rights of the student. In addition, a tort differs from a crime in several ways, which are listed below.

 **DEFINITIONS**

tort
a civil (or private), noncontractual wrong for which a court will award damages to an injured party

❑ A tort is an offense against an individual (a private wrong); a crime is an offense against the state (a public wrong).

❑ A tort action is initiated by the injured party (in this case, the student or the parents or guardians of the student); a criminal action is initiated by the state.

❑ In a tort action, the rights of the injured party are created by statute or precedent (previous court cases); in a criminal action, the rights of the injured party are created by statute.

There are three main categories of torts: negligence, intentional interference, and strict liability. Negligent torts are the most common.

What is a negligent tort?

If an accident occurs and a student is injured, the student or the parents or guardians of the student may sue you (and your administration) in the form of a negligent tort lawsuit. In such a lawsuit, the court uses fault instead of intent as the basis for imposing liability. The following four elements must be established to prove liability.

❑ **A legal duty of care** Duty is the behavioral baseline upon which the negligent tort is based and is an obligation recognized by the court as the minimum acceptable standard of conduct. If there is no legal duty between the parties involved, there is no negligence.

Standard of care is difficult to determine—there are no precise definitions for care, so this topic is often discussed during a trial. An appropriate standard of care is determined by weighing the inherent risks of an activity against the pedagogic value of the activity and the probability of injury caused by the behavior (or lack of behavior) of the teacher. If the standard of care is not set by statute, then the standard used by the court is that of reasonable care.

Reasonable care is the prudence of the "reasonable person," which is a legal construction. A reasonable person is expected to be aware of the variability of human nature and anticipate ordinary possible events. In some cases, even extraordinary events should be anticipated by the reasonable person. Prudence is decided based on what the facts of the case are and how these facts apply to previous court cases or how other teachers in similar situations would act (based on the testimony of expert witnesses).

- ❑ **A breach of legal duty of care** Breach is established when a teacher is shown to have acted below the prevailing standard of care.

- ❑ **The cause or proximate cause of the breach** The cause of the injury must also be established by the court. There are two standards to use in evaluating cause.

    - ❑ **Cause in fact** This phrase means that the negligent action itself was the reason for the accident or the direct cause of the injury.

    - ❑ **Proximate cause** This phrase means that the negligent action initiated a chain of events that led to the accident or that led to the indirect or legal cause of the injury. The two categories of proximate cause are as follows:

        - ❑ **Foreseeability** Foreseeability is negligence due to a failure on the part of the negligent party to determine a potential for harm that reasonably prudent teachers would have anticipated.

        - ❑ **Intervening cause** Intervening cause is an act or event that occurs subsequent to the teacher's act and before the injury.

- ❑ **Damages** If the previous elements are established, then the injured student may recover damages. Damages are the monetary award set by a judge or jury.

Usually, the issues of breach and damages in a negligent tort lawsuit are not debated; however, duty and cause are often disputable. Unfortunately, no absolute criteria for establishing a negligent tort exist. As a result, each case must be analyzed individually.

What defenses do I have if I am accused of negligence?

If you are accused of negligence, you have several defenses, each of which has advantages and disadvantages. Commonly used defenses include the following:

❏ **Contributory negligence** This defense is a limited defense because it requires a teacher to prove that the student's own unreasonable behavior or conduct contributed significantly to the student's injury. In addition, courts do not hold young students to the same standard of care as they hold adults to. The younger the student, the more difficult to make use of this defense. However, if a student is shown to be at least partially negligent, then the negligence of the teacher may be excused or decreased.

❏ **Assumption of risk** The basis of this defense is that the teacher's negligence is excused because of the student's voluntary consent to encounter the hazard resulting from an activity. This defense is extremely hard to use successfully because students are considered a "captive audience"—they must complete activities as requirements of the class. The key to this defense is proving that injured students must have known about any risks inherent in the activity. Risks cannot be assumed by the students if the students are ignorant of the dangers. Furthermore, only the reasonable risks that are normally associated with the activity can be assumed by the students. The defendant has the burden of proof in this defense.

Less common defenses that can be used in a case of a negligent tort include the following:

❏ **Comparative negligence** This defense allows for a scaled establishment of negligence and a proportional adjustment of damages. Concern for students injured in classrooms led many states to enact statutes setting degrees of negligence and damages. For example, if a court finds each party was 50 percent responsible, then the student or students would be awarded one-half the usual amount of damages. In other cases, even if contributory negligence by the teacher is established, the teacher may be absolved of all liability if others are shown to be more responsible for the accident.

❑ **Bar by statute of limitations** The basis for this defense is that an applicable statute of limitations has expired, so the case cannot come to court. However, the statute of limitations seldom expires for a negligent tort which is serious enough for court consideration. Also, many risks in education are not covered by specific statutes, so this defense often cannot be used.

❑ **Immunity** This defense is usually used to protect school districts against liability. In the past, school districts were not held liable when accidents occurred in the classroom, but teachers were. Fortunately, many states have rejected this defense and allowed school districts to be sued. These states have also created "save harmless" provisions to protect teachers against liability up to a specified amount of damages. These provisions act as a sort of liability insurance for teachers.

Other defenses include "Act of God" (the injury resulted from natural causes) or "Denial" (claim no responsibility for the cause of the injury or loss). These defenses are rarely useful in classroom situations.

What about insurance?

Private insurance is another form of liability protection. School districts have liability coverage as well as legal assistance. While these provisions are very helpful, remember that the face amount of the monetary coverage is the total available to all parties named in a lawsuit. The coverage is usually divided equally among the parties, and the coverage that initially seemed substantial can be split so many ways that it becomes inconsequential in aiding you during a lawsuit.

Private insurance may be purchased to supplement your school district's coverage. Typically, professional or business coverage can be purchased as a rider to a homeowner policy. However, the cost for this coverage is usually expensive.

You should also note that insurance does not replace or compensate for safe practices in your classroom. You should ensure the safety of everyone in your classroom before injuries occur and not wait until after injuries occur to improve conditions.

CHAPTER 10

Final words

Note that the discussion in this chapter is not exhaustive and gives you only a few of the key concepts of your legal responsibilities as a teacher and a few of the defenses you could use if you were sued. To help ensure that you are doing all you can to prevent injury in your classroom, follow these guidelines on legal compliance:

 **SAFETY INFORMATION**

This list of guidelines is taken from *Better Science Through Safety*, by Jack Gerlovich and Gary Downs. See the appendix for more information.

❑ Protect the safety, health, and welfare of your students.

❑ Foresee the reasonable consequences of your students' actions (or inaction).

❑ Be in the classroom and attentive while activities are in progress.

❑ Instruct your students in the use of equipment.

❑ Carefully instruct your students about the risks inherent in activities.

❑ Modify such instruction to compensate for the age and maturity of your students.

❑ Maintain appropriate behavior.

❑ Immediately address or report hazardous conditions.

Additional Issues

What should I know about demonstrations?

Demonstrations expose students to and interest students in different areas of science. Therefore, many demonstrators often make their demonstrations very dramatic to attract attention. These dramatic demonstrations are sometimes necessary; however, demonstrators often place more value on drama than on education. The value of demonstrations should be based primarily on pedagogic value. Entertainment should be a secondary concern. Both learning and entertainment can safely occur during a demonstration, but be careful of the message your demonstration sends. You do not want your audience to think that science is only fun when it is explosive or seemingly dangerous.

How do you evaluate the relationship between the pedagogic value and the entertainment value of a demonstration? Applying the risk analysis method discussed earlier will be helpful in making this assessment. In addition, the following tips may help you determine if a demonstration should be used in your classroom.

✔ Make sure that the demonstration is safe to perform for both you and your audience.

✔ Remember that your students may try to repeat a demonstration at home, so tell your students of any hazards a demonstration may have, and fully explain each demonstration.

✔ Make sure that a demonstration has pedagogic value. Demonstrations that only astound and amaze should not be performed. These demonstrations give students an inaccurate impression of science and are often dangerous.

What should I know about outside activities?

Outside activities are any activity or project conducted outside the classroom. These activities may not be supervised by you, another teacher, or a chaperone. Examples of outside activities are science-fair projects, some homework, activities that are completed in other parts of the school, and activities that are performed in places such as amusement parks. Listed below are some considerations to help you decide if an activity is safe and appropriate.

✔ Planning

✔ You must be extremely careful when your students perform experiments and activities outside your classroom because much thought and planning are necessary to minimize risk. When you consider an activity or experiment, remember the following questions.

✔ Scope

✔ What are the goals and objectives of the activity?

✔ **Target group**

> ✔ Are your students capable of performing the activity? How sophisticated are your students?

✔ **Risk analysis**

> ✔ What are the risks of the activity? Which risks can be eliminated, and which can be minimized?

✔ **Legal issues**

> ✔ Does the activity conform to applicable federal, state, and local regulations? What is my liability if an accident occurs while this activity is performed?

✔ **Materials**

> ✔ Did you give your students clear, concise written and oral instructions for using the materials? Have you explained to your students the hazards of the activity?

 **SAFE LABS**

Approve your students' science-fair project ideas before your students perform them. By approving your students' projects, you will be able to reject any ideas that are dangerous and you may be able to prevent accidents.

✔ **Supervision**

> ✔ Consider the following questions before your students perform an activity.
>
> > ✔ Will you or a chaperone monitor the activity?
> >
> > ✔ Do the chaperones and students know their responsibilities?
> >
> > ✔ How will you evaluate your students' performance during or after an activity? Will students make daily or occasional reports?
> >
> > ✔ What instructions will be given before and during the activity? Will these instructions be written or oral?
> >
> > ✔ How will students know if they are performing the activity correctly?
>
> ✔ Emphasize safety before and during the activity.
>
> ✔ Remember that the degree of supervision should be commensurate with the difficulty of the activity as well as with the abilities of your students.

✔ **Legal Issues**

> ✔ See chapter "Legal Issues" for a detailed discussion of your liability.
>
> ✔ Remember to document the actions you took to ensure the safety of your students.

✔ Have the parents of your students who participate in off-site activities sign waiver forms. These forms are usually required for a student to participate in an activity and show that certain steps were taken to ensure the safety of your students. However, these forms will not absolve you of your liability if an accident occurs. Courts have held that a "captive audience" (students who must perform an activity if they want to pass the class) cannot "sign away," or yield, their legal rights.

✔ To protect you, your students, and others, consider carefully the pedagogy and the risks of an activity.

What should I know about the Americans with Disabilities Act (ADA)?

The Americans with Disabilities Act bans the discrimination of and provides equal opportunity for anyone with disabilities. According to this act, you must make every effort to provide reasonable accommodations for any person with a disability. Reasonable accommodations can include providing a desk-height portable table or rescheduling, redesigning, or providing more time to do an activity. You are obligated to revise all activities to provide reasonable accommodations, unless in your *carefully reasoned analysis,* you discover that an activity cannot be revised so that it can be safely performed by a person with a disability. The analysis used to make this decision should include documentable reasons or incontrovertible proof that supports your decisions. In addition, you should make an effort to include the student with a disability even if the person is incapable of performing the activity.

All teachers must comply with the Individuals with Disabilities Education Act (IDEA). A provision of this act is the development of an appropriate Individualized Education Program (IEP) for each eligible student. This program should include input from teachers, parents, the student, and special-education professionals. Appropriate levels of participation in laboratory activities by the student with a disability can be determined in the course of creating the IEP. Students with disabilities should participate in the creation of these programs because they best know what they can and cannot do. Their participation also allows them to know what will be expected of them. More tips are listed below.

✔ Schedule a special orientation session before the school year to allow students with disabilities to become familiar with facilities and learn about the activities that they will perform.

✔ Provide special handouts. Depending on the specific disability, these handouts could have large print or Braille and could include more diagrams and pictures.

CHAPTER 11

✔ Provide additional instruction or discussion for students with disabilities.

✔ Ensure that students with disabilities are stationed close to exits and safety equipment.

✔ Arrange to have other students assist students with disabilities during evacuations.

✔ Encourage students with disabilities to wear protective equipment.

✔ Adjust your teaching style to accommodate students with disabilities. For example, use more visual cues, write in large print, and talk more slowly or louder.

✔ Allow more time for students with disabilities to finish activities.

What should I know about the facilities of my school?

Teachers are generally not responsible for the maintenance of their classrooms. However, you must be aware of the condition of your facilities so that you can report these potential or existing hazards to the proper maintenance authorities. Examples of types of hazards include the following.

❑ **Physical**—the uncleanness of your classroom and equipment storage, slippery floors, or malfunctioning or broken locks or windows

❑ **Mechanical**—malfunctioning hoods, air handlers, air conditioners, or heaters

❑ **Electrical**—overheating of equipment or damaged outlets

❑ **Pressure**—leaking natural gas lines or gases under pressure

❑ **Chemical**—spilled or leaking chemicals

❑ **Noise**—the vibration of a loose or misaligned part, an equipment hum, or a background noise

❑ **Thermal**—fire hazards, unsafe storage of flammables, or spilled combustibles

Not doing anything about hazardous conditions exposes you, students, and other staff members to danger. Inaction also creates liability, especially if courts establish that you knew about the unsafe conditions of your classroom. The following list contains other issues of which you should be aware.

✔ Facilities, which are ordinarily safe, can be hazardous if used for unsuitable activities. Science classes should not be held in classrooms that are not equipped for science experiments. Official protests should be filed in writing if facilities are to be used improperly.

✔ Overcrowded classrooms are especially hazardous. The number of laboratory accidents tends to increase as enrollment increases. What would happen if there were a fire and 50 students tried to escape from a room meant for 35?

 SAFETY INFORMATION

The National Science Teachers Association (NSTA), has published *The NSTA Guide to School Science Facilities* which provides a thorough discussion about safe facilities.

✔ Classrooms should not be open to the public. Someone walking into your classroom may startle students or expose them to a hazardous situation. Visitors should be allowed in your classroom only when you have met them at the door and students have been notified in advance. If appropriate for the activity you and your students are performing, give each visitor protective equipment, such as goggles.

✔ You may help develop a facility renovation or new construction. Make sure that the new facilities will permit you to do your job safely.

What should I know about model rockets?

Launching rockets is a popular activity at many schools. If you are considering such an activity, you must consider several things, such as the following:

✔ school system regulations regarding the use of model rockets

✔ Federal Aviation Administration (FAA) restrictions in the area

✔ prospective launch sites

✔ fire codes

If students are to construct their own rockets, follow the tips below.

✔ Instruct students on the proper use of tools when they construct rockets (for example, X-acto knives and Dremel tools).

✔ Construct rockets from lightweight materials.

✔ Use only factory-made engines. Do not alter these engines, try to reuse them, or have students make their own engines.

✔ Test homemade rocket designs for reliability and stability before launching them.

CHAPTER 11

Before you launch any rockets, consider the following tips.

✔ Do not establish a launch site near buildings, trees, power lines, or any other obstruction.

✔ Do not launch rockets if high winds, lightning, low-flying planes, or any other threatening conditions are near the launch site.

✔ Always inspect rockets before launch to ensure that no rocket has an unauthorized payload.

✔ The launch area must be clear of obstructions and combustible materials.

✔ All rockets must have deflectors so that engine exhaust does not strike the ground directly.

✔ Warn students to be careful while working around the launch rod.

✔ Use a launch rod that is taller than all of your students.

✔ The launch system must be electrically controlled and have a momentary-contact on-off switch.

✔ Keep all observers at least 10 ft away from the launch pad.

When you or your students recover rockets, always use care and never try to recover rockets stuck in power lines, behind security fences, or in any dangerous or unauthorized areas.

APPENDIX A: Bibliography

Alexander, K., and M. D. Alexander., *The Law of Schools, Students, and Teachers.* St. Paul, Minn.: West Publishing Co., 1984.

American Chemical Society Committee of Chemical Safety. *Safety in Academic Chemistry Laboratories.* 6th ed. Washington, D.C.: American Chemical Society, 1995.

American National Standards Institute. "American National Standard for Laboratory Ventilation, Z9.5." New York, N.Y.: American National Standards Institute. Current edition.

American National Standards Institute. "American National Standard for the Safe Use of Lasers: ANSI Z136.1-1986." Orlando, Fla.: Laser Institute of America, 1986.

American National Standards Institute. "Emergency Eyewash and Shower Equipment, Z358.1." New York, N.Y.: American National Standards Institute. Current edition.

American National Standards Institute. "Practice for Occupational and Educational Eye and Face Protection: ANSI Z87.1." New York: American National Standards Institute. Current edition.

American National Standards Institute. "Safety Levels with Respect to Human Exposure to Radio Frequency Electromagnetic Fields, 300 kHz to 100 GHz: ANSI C95.1." New York, N.Y.: American National Standards Institute, 1999.

American Red Cross. *Standard First Aid Workbook.* St. Louis, Mo.: Mosby-Year Book, Inc., 1992.

American Red Cross. *Standard First Aid and Personal Safety.* 2nd ed. Garden City, N.Y.: Doubleday, 1981.

Americans with Disabilities Act. *Individuals with Educational Disabilities, 34CFR Part 300,* Washington, D.C.: U.S. Government Printing Office, July 2001.

Biehle, James T., LaMoine L. Motz, and Sandra S. West. *The NSTA Guide to School Science Facilities.* Arlington, Va.: NSTA Press Publications, 1999.

Brown, B. W. and W. R. Brown. *Science Teaching and the Law.* Washington, D.C.: National Science Teachers Association, 1969.

Budavari, Susan, ed. *The Merck Index.* 12th ed. Rahway, NJ: Merck and Co., 1996.

Cohen, S. and N. Weinstein. "Nonauditory Effects of Noise on Behavior and Health." *Journal of Social Issues* 37 (1981): 36–70.

Compressed Gas Association. *Handbook of Compressed Gases.* 3rd ed. New York, N.Y.: Van Nostrand Reinhold, 1990.

Council Committee of Chemical Safety. *Safety in Academic Chemistry Laboratories.* 5th ed. Washington, D.C.: American Chemical Society, 1995.

Dalziel, Charles. "The Effects of Electric Shock on Man." *Safety and Fire Protection Technical Bulletin: no. 7.* Washington, D.C.: U.S. Atomic Energy Commission, Office of Health and Safety, 1956.

Dezettel, Louis M. *Electrical Soldering.* Indianapolis, Ind.: Sams & Co., 1976.

Dulbecco, Renato, ed. *Encyclopedia of Human Biology.* Vol. 4. San Diego, Calif.: Academic Press Inc., 1991.

Furr, Keith A., ed. *CRC Handbook of Laboratory Safety.* 5th ed. Boca Raton, Fla.: CRC Press, 2001.

Garcia, Rosendo. Presentation. "Safety is My Middle Name." Seventh ACT$_2$ Welch Biennial Conference, Belton, Tex., 26 June 2001.

Geddes, Leslie A., ed. *Handbook of Electrical Hazards and Accidents.* Boca Raton, Fla.: CRC Press, 1995.

Gerlovich, Jack and Gary Downs. *Better Science Through Safety.* Ames, Iowa: Iowa State University Press, 1981.

Gerlovich, J. A., et al. *School Science Safety.* Batavia, Ill.: Flinn Scientific, Inc., 1984.

Goleman, D. "Hidden Rules Often Distort Ideas of Risk." *New York Times* 1 Feb. 1994, Science section.

Grose, Vernon L. *Managing Risk: Systematic Loss and Prevention for Executives.* Englewood Cliffs, N.J.: Prentice Hall, 1987.

Hall, S. K. *Chemical Safety in the Laboratory.* Boca Raton, Fla.: Lewis Publishers, 1994.

Hallenbeck, William H. *Radiation Protection.* Boca Raton, Fla.: Lewis Publishers, 1994.

Lefevre, M. J. *First Aid Manual for Chemical Accidents.* 2nd ed. New York: Van Nostrand Reinhold, 1989.

Lewis, Richard J. *Hazardous Chemical Desk Reference.* 3rd ed. New York, N.Y.: Van Nostrand Reinhold, 1993.

MacCrimmon, R. Kenneth and Donald A. Wehrung. *Taking Risks: The Management of Uncertainty.* New York, N.Y.: The Free Press, 1986.

Mahn, William J. *Fundamentals of Laboratory Safety: Physical Hazards in the Academic Laboratory.* New York, N.Y.: Van Nostrand Reinhold, 1991.

Mercier, Paul. *Laboratory Safety Pocket Guide.* Schenectady, N.Y.: Genium Publishing Corporation, 1996.

Miller, Brinton, ed., et. al. *Laboratory Safety: Principles and Practices.* Washington, D.C.: American Society for Microbiology, 1986.

Moore, J. H., C. C. Davis, and M. A. Coplan. *Building Scientific Apparatus.* Reading, Mass.: Addison-Wesley Publishing Co., 1983.

Morrison, Ralph. *Ground and Shielding Techniques in Instrumentation.* 2nd ed., New York, N.Y.: John Wiley and Sons, 1977.

National Council on Radiation Protection and Measurements. "Limitations of Exposure to Ionizing Radiation." Report #116. 1993.

National Fire Protection Association. "Fire Protection for Laboratories Using Chemicals." Quincy, Mass.: National Fire Protection Association, current edition.

National Fire Protection Association. *NFPA Fire Protection Guide on Hazardous Materials.* 11th ed. Quincy, Mass.: National Fire Protection Association, 1994.

National Research Council. *Prudent Practices for Handling Hazardous Chemicals in Laboratories.* Washington D.C.: National Academy Press, 1981.

National Research Council. *Prudent Practices for Handling Hazardous Chemicals in Laboratories.* Washington D.C.: National Academy Press, 1983.

Nuclear Regulatory Commission. 10CFR Parts 0-199. Washington, D.C.: U.S. Government Printing Office, 2001.

Occupational Safety and Health Administration. *Occupational Safety and Health Standards 29CFR Parts 1900–end.* Washington, D.C.: U.S. Government Printing Office, 2001.

Pipitone, D. A. and D. Hedberg. "Safe Chemical Storage." *Journal of Chemical Education.* 59 (1982): A159.

Reese, K. M. *Health and Safety Guidelines for Chemistry Teachers.* Washington, D.C.: American Chemical Society, 1980.

Sax, N. I. and R. J. Lewis, Sr. *Hazardous Chemicals Desk Reference.* New York, N.Y.: Van Nostrand Reinhold, 1987.

Shugar, J. Gershon and Jack T. Ballinger. *Chemical Technicians Ready Reference Handbook.* 4th ed. New York, N.Y.: Mc Graw-Hill Inc., 1996.

Sliney, David H. and Myron L. Wolbarsh. *Safety With Lasers and Other Optical Sources.* New York, N.Y.: Plenum Press, 1980.

Steere, V. Norman, ed. *CRC Handbook of Laboratory Safety.* 2nd ed. Cleveland, Ohio: The Chemical Rubber Co., 1971.

Varian Vacuum Products. *Basic Vacuum Practice.* 3rd ed. Lexington, Mass.: Varian Associates, Inc., 1992.

Young, Jay A. "Risk Assessment and Hazard Evaluation for Undergraduate Laboratory Experiments." *Journal of Chemical Education* 59 (1982): A265.

Young, Jay A., ed. *Improving Safety in the Chemical Laboratory: A Practical Guide.* 2nd ed. New York, N.Y.: Wiley InterScience, 1991.

Zabatekis, Michael G. *Safety with Cryogenic Fluid.* New York, N.Y.: Plenum Press, 1967.

APPENDIX B: Emergency Procedures for Some Common Cases

Tips for handling some accidents, emergencies, and situations are listed in this section. You should obtain CPR and basic first aid training so that you can help treat almost any injury or condition that may occur in your classroom.

Sudden illness

Not all emergencies are the result of major accidents. You may have an emergency in your classroom in which a student is ill. The most common example of an illness that a student can have is fainting. However, you may also encounter students that have chronic illnesses, such as heart disease, and epilepsy. People with chronic illnesses often wear medic alert bracelets, which describe their condition and the first-aid steps to perform in case of emergency. You should ask your students during the first class meeting to privately see you if they have a medical condition.

Fainting

Several symptoms characterize fainting and include extreme paleness, sweating, cold and clammy skin, dizziness, and nausea. If a student faints in your classroom or school, you should perform the following steps.

- ✔ Leave the person who has fainted lying down.
- ✔ Loosen any tight clothing on the person.
- ✔ Make sure that the person has an open air passageway.
- ✔ Do not give the person any liquids.
- ✔ Call for emergency medical assistance.

Epilepsy

Epilepsy is characterized by disturbed electrical rhythms of the central nervous system and encompasses many disorders. Severe epilepsy is characterized by repeated, violent convulsions. A person who has a milder form of epilepsy has no convulsions but may experience brief twitchings of muscles and a reduction in the awareness of his or her surroundings. Unfortunately, the severe form of epilepsy is more common than the milder form of epilepsy. If someone has an epileptic episode, you should follow the steps below.

- ✔ Remove any objects near the person who is experiencing an epileptic episode. Do not restrain the person.
- ✔ Do not force anything between the person's teeth.
- ✔ Loosen clothing around the person's neck after the person has stopped convulsing.
- ✔ Keep the person lying down.
- ✔ Make sure that the person has an open air passageway.
- ✔ If the person stops breathing, perform artificial respiration.

✔ Allow the person to sleep or rest after the epileptic episode.

✔ Get emergency medical assistance.

If you know a person has epilepsy, you may not have to get emergency medical assistance if arrangements had been reached prior to the epileptic episode. If an epileptic episode lasts longer than a few minutes, another episode occurs soon after the first, or the person does not regain consciousness after the episode, you should get emergency medical assistance.

Seizures (other than those caused by epilepsy)

Seizures may be caused by a temporary illness, such as insulin shock, high fever, viral infections that affect the brain, head injuries, or drug reactions. Symptoms of seizures include a person having an aura (sensation) before the onset of the seizure. Auras can be aural and visual hallucinations, a strange taste in the mouth, abdominal pain, numbness, or a sense of urgency to move to safety.

Seizures can be mild or severe. Characteristics of seizures are brief blackouts, involuntary movements, sudden falls, periods of confused behavior, and convulsions. Severe seizures may involve uncontrollable jerking, spasms, rigidity, loss of consciousness, loss of bladder and bowel control, and, in some cases, temporary cessation of breathing. You should perform the same steps for a person who is having a seizure as for a person who is having an epileptic episode.

✔ Remove any objects near the person who is experiencing a seizure. Do not restrain the person.

✔ Do not force anything between the person's teeth.

✔ Loosen clothing around the person's neck after the person has stopped seizing.

✔ Keep the person lying down.

✔ Make sure that the person has an open air passageway.

✔ If the person stops breathing, perform artificial respiration.

✔ Allow the person to sleep or rest after the seizure.

✔ Get emergency medical assistance.

A person is likely to be drowsy and disoriented after having a seizure. The person will need rest and reassurance. Stay with the person until he or she is fully conscious and aware.

Eye injuries

Eye injuries can be blunt or penetrating. A blunt injury, or contusion, of the eye often occurs from a severe direct blow, such as a hit from a fist or debris from an explosion. In serious blunt injuries to the eye, some tissue of the eye may be torn or ruptured. More damage to the eye may be produced by the effects of a hemorrhage or by infection. A penetrating injury of the eye is extremely serious. If an object penetrates or lacerates the eyeball, a loss of vision or even blindness can result.

If someone suffers from an injury to the eyelid, follow the steps below.

✔ Stop any bleeding by gently applying direct pressure to the eyelid with a bandage or handkerchief.

✔ Apply a sterile dressing to the eyelid.

✔ Call emergency medical assistance.

If someone suffers from a blunt injury or contusion to the eye, follow the steps below.

✔ Apply a dry, sterile dressing to both eyes (movement of the undamaged eye will cause the damaged eye to move and possibly cause more damage).

✔ Call emergency medical assistance.

If someone suffers from a penetrating injury to the eye, follow the steps below.

✔ Do not remove the object or wash the eye.

✔ Cover both eyes to prevent eye movement. Avoid making the covering so tight that pressure is put on the affected eye. If possible, cover the injured eye with a paper cup and wrap the dressing around the base of the cup to hold it in place.

✔ Call emergency medical assistance.

If someone suffers from a chemical burn to the eye, follow the steps below.

✔ Wash the affected eye with lots of running water by flushing from the nose outward for 15 to 30 min.

✔ Wrap a bandage around both eyes.

✔ Call emergency medical assistance.

Diabetic emergencies (insulin reactions)

Blood carries sugar to cells of the body for nourishment. Insulin is a hormone that helps the cells assimilate sugar. When a person does not produce enough insulin to make sugar available for his or her cells, the person may develop diabetes. A person can control diabetes by taking medication and regulating diet and exercise.

A person may experience an insulin reaction when the person has too much insulin and not enough sugar in the body which causes a rapid reduction of the person's blood-sugar level. Insulin reactions can be caused by taking too much medication, failing to eat, by exercising heavily, or experiencing emotional stress. Symptoms of insulin reaction are fast breathing, fast pulse, dizziness, weakness, loss of consciousness or decrease in awareness, visual difficulties, sweating, headache, numb hands or feet, and hunger. Insulin shock is an emergency, so it requires a quick response. You can treat insulin reaction by giving the affected person candy, fruit, a soft drink that contains sugar, or a glass of water that has a packet of sugar dissolved in it. (Note: NutraSweet® or other artificial sweeteners will not work.) If the person who has had the insulin reaction is unconscious, call emergency medical assistance as soon as possible.

Nosebleeds

If a person is bleeding from one or both nostrils, treat this injury by following the steps below.

✔ Loosen clothing around the neck area of the person who has the nosebleed. Instruct the person to sit up with her or his head tilted forward or to lie down with head and shoulders elevated.

✔ Instruct the person to breathe through the mouth.

✔ If the bleeding is from the front of the nose, pinch the nostrils together for 5 min and place cold, wet towels or cloths over the face and nose.

✔ If bleeding continues, insert a small sterile pad in one or both nostrils. Make sure the pad extends from the nostril. Pinch nostrils together. If bleeding continues, get emergency medical assistance.

✔ If bleeding is from the back of the nose, get emergency medical assistance immediately.

Bleeding

There are three types of bleeding.

❏ **Arterial bleeding**
This type of bleeding is the loss of blood from an artery, which carries oxygen-rich blood from the heart throughout the body. Arterial bleeding is characterized by blood spurting from the wound with each heartbeat and by the bright red color of the blood. This type of bleeding is usually severe, hard to control, and requires immediate emergency medical assistance.

❏ **Venous bleeding**
Venous bleeding is the loss of blood from a vein, which carries blood without oxygen back to the heart. The type of bleeding occurs in a steady flow, which can be heavy. The blood from this type of bleeding is dark red. Venous bleeding is easier to control than arterial bleeding, but emergency medical assistance is necessary.

❏ **Capillary bleeding**
This type of bleeding is the loss of blood from capillaries, which are the smallest blood vessels. The blood flow of this type of bleeding is usually slow, but the person who experiences capillary bleeding has a greater risk of infection than a person who experiences one of the other types of bleeding.

A person can have external or internal bleeding. External bleeding is caused by open wounds, which are injuries in which the skin is torn. Several types of open wounds occur. A few of these types are described below.

❑ **Abrasions**

Abrasions are damage to the skin from a scrape by a hard surface. These injuries result in little bleeding and can cause infection.

❑ **Incisions**

These injuries are caused by sharp, even cuts from knives, broken glass, or other sharp objects. Incisions can cause heavy bleeding and damage to muscles, tendons, and nerves.

❑ **Lacerations**

These injuries are jagged or torn soft tissues, which are usually caused by objects, that have sharp, irregular edges or by forces exerted against the body. Tissue damage is greater for lacerations than for incisions.

❑ **Punctures**

Punctures are small holes in tissue and are caused by bullets and pointed objects such as pins, nails, and splinters and produce little external bleeding. A person who has a puncture wound could have internal bleeding or get an infection, such as tetanus.

❑ **Avulsions**

Avulsions are tissues that are torn or hang from the body and produce heavy bleeding. These injuries result from accidents with motor vehicles or machinery, explosions, and animal bites. In many cases, the skin can be reattached by a surgeon.

Internal bleeding can cause small bruises or injuries serious enough to cause shock, heart failure, or lung failure. Internal bleeding can also result from crushing injuries, punctures, injuries from blunt objects, bruised tissues, and fractured bones. Symptoms are

❑ bruised, swollen, tender, or rigid abdomen

❑ bruises on the chest or signs of fractured ribs

❑ blood in vomit

❑ wounds that have penetrated the chest or abdomen

❑ abnormal pulse and difficult breathing

❑ cool, moist skin

First aid for external bleeding includes stopping the bleeding and preventing infection and shock. Specific steps are listed below.

✔ Call for emergency medical assistance.

✔ Place a sterile dressing over the wound and apply pressure. This action is the most effective treatment. If a sterile dressing is not available, use a handkerchief or, as a last resort, use your bare hand. The purpose of the dressing is to absorb blood and permit the blood to clot. Do not remove a dressing if it becomes blood soaked; just apply another dressing on top of the first dressing and keep pressure on the wound.

✔ If the injured person also has injuries such as a fracture or potential spinal cord damage, do not move the injured person. If the injured person has no such injuries, then elevate the wound so that it is higher than the heart. This action reduces the blood pressure in the area of the wound.

✔ If bleeding cannot be stopped by direct pressure, you will have to try putting pressure on a main artery supplying blood to the area. This is done by compressing the artery, which is between the wound and the heart, against a bone. Note that if this technique is used too long, additional injuries can occur to the area beyond the compression point. Use of this technique should be discontinued as soon as possible, unless this technique is the only effective technique.

✔ As a last resort, apply a tourniquet to stop the bleeding. The tourniquet should be at least 2 in. wide. You will need to note the time the tourniquet was applied and tell emergency personnel arrive when they arrive so that they can perform the proper actions.

Remember that a relatively small amount of blood can look dramatic. Do not get so concerned by the amount of blood that you overlook other injuries a person may have. Bleeding can also frighten the person who is injured, so try to reassure the person.

To reduce the threat of infection to the injured person as well as to yourself, wear latex gloves. If possible, wash your hands before and after caring for a wound. Use clean dressings and bandages to treat an injured person. Wash minor wounds that are not bleeding severely with soap and water before applying the dressing (do not clean major wounds that are bleeding severely).

First aid for internal bleeding is listed below.

✔ If the injury is a simple bruise, apply cold packs (but do not apply ice directly) to the area to prevent swelling and to slow internal bleeding.

✔ If you suspect a more serious internal injury, get emergency medical assistance immediately. While waiting for help, monitor vital signs (which indicate breathing and circulation) of the person, reassure the person, control any external bleeding, and care for shock.

Head and back injuries

If you suspect a neck or back injury, do not move the person unless the person's life will be threatened. Call for emergency medical assistance. If the person seems dazed or disoriented, keep the person immobile until emergency medical assistance arrives.

Shock

Whenever a person experiences a severe injury, such as a heart attack, loss of blood, or burns, you must watch for the onset of shock. Shock is the failure of the cardiovascular system to keep an adequate supply of blood circulating to the vital organs. It develops as a result of the body's attempts to correct damage from severe injury. Shock has several noticeable characteristics: the skin becomes cold to the touch and may become clammy and turn a pale or bluish color, the pulse weakens and becomes rapid, pupils enlarge, and breathing becomes rapid and irregular. A person who is in shock may become very weak, restless, thirsty, and unresponsive. Dilation of the eyes may occur. To treat shock, follow the steps below.

✔ Get emergency medical assistance.

✔ The person who is in shock should be lying down to improve circulation. However, the best position for the person depends on the type of injury. If you are uncertain of the best position, let the person lie on his or her back with the feet raised 20 to 30 cm (only if the person is not in pain when her or his feet are raised). If you suspect the person has a head, neck or back injury, let the person lie flat. Do not move the person unless hazards are in the immediate area.

✔ Cover the person with coats or other clothing to keep the person warm. However, do not try to heat the person by using heaters or other devices.

✔ If the person is conscious and not vomiting, then give the person approximately half a glassful of liquid (for example, water or soda) about every 15 min. Do not give liquids if the person is unconscious or nauseated. If the person vomits, place the person to one side to allow fluids to drain from her or his mouth.

✔ If the person has trouble breathing, place the person in a semi reclined position by using boxes or coats to support the head or back. This position will make breathing easier for the person.

Burns

Heat, chemicals, or electricity can cause burns. The severity of a burn depends on its depth, size, and the location of the burn on the body. Burns are most serious when they are located on the face, neck, hands, feet, or genitals; when they are spread over large areas of the body; or when other injuries are also present. Shock and infection can result from burns.

Burns are classified according to their depth or degree. The deeper the burn, the more severe it is. The following list describes the types of burns (see the chapter entitled Thermal Hazards for more information).

❑ **First-degree burns**
First-degree burns are the least severe type of burn. These burns are characterized by redness or discoloration, mild swelling, and pain. They

affect only the epidermis (first layer) of the skin and are usually the result of light contact with hot objects, minor scalding by water or steam, or brief contact with chemicals.

❑ **Second-degree burns**

Second-degree burns are deeper than first-degree burns in that they affect the dermis (second layer of skin) as well as the epidermis. These burns look red or mottled and have blisters. They may also look wet from the loss of fluid through the damaged skin. Second-degree burns can result from contact with hot liquids or flash burns from objects bursting into flame. These burns are often the most painful type of burn because nerve endings are still intact despite the tissue damage.

❑ **Third-degree burns**

Third-degree burns are the deepest type of burn as they affect the full thickness of the skin and possibly even subcutaneous tissue, such as muscle or bone. This type of burn may look white or charred, or it can look like a second-degree burn. Third-degree burns are most frequently caused by clothing that has ignited, immersion of tissue in hot water, or contact with flames, hot objects, or electricity. The burned person may complain of severe pain, but if nerve endings are destroyed, the person may feel little pain.

If someone suffers from a burn caused by heat, follow the steps below.

✔ For a person who has first-degree burns or second-degree burns without open blisters, flush the burns of the injured person with lots of cool (not cold) running water. Apply moist dressings and bandage loosely. Call for emergency medical assistance.

✔ For a person who has second-degree burns with open blisters or third-degree burns, call emergency medical assistance. Then, apply dry dressings and bandage loosely to the person's burns. Do not use water as a treatment because it increases the chance of the person experiencing shock.

If someone suffers from a burn caused by chemicals, follow the steps below.

✔ Call for emergency medical assistance.

✔ Use lots of running water to flush chemicals from the skin (15 to 30 min), and remove any clothing and jewelry on which chemicals have spilled.

✔ Cover burns with dry, loose dressings.

✔ Be aware of the possibility of the burned person experiencing shock.

APPENDIX B

If someone suffers from a burn caused by electricity, follow the steps below.

✔ Be careful not to get shocked by electricity. Turn off the source of the electricity or remove the source of electricity from the victim by using an insulating device (wooden meter stick or broom handle). Keep bystanders away from the sources of electricity.

✔ Call for emergency medical assistance.

✔ Check the burned person for more than one burn. Cover all burns with dry, loose dressings, and then bandage the dressings.

✔ Be aware that the burned person may experience cardiac arrest or shock.

Respiratory injuries

If a person has inhaled a toxic gas or has been exposed to high levels of an asphyxiant, he or she should be removed to fresh air as quickly as possible. Close the gas source, and admit fresh air into the room, if necessary and if possible. However, do not move an injured person if this action will expose you or another person to the same conditions that affected the injured person. Self-contained breathing apparatus may be necessary to assist the injured person; however, if you are not trained in the proper use of such equipment, you should not attempt to use it. Remember to call for emergency medical assistance.

APPENDIX C: Emergency Evacuation Procedures

1. If you and your students must evacuate your classroom, lead your students to the nearest exit or stairway. Stairwells are barriers for smoke if fire doors are kept closed and should be fire resistant.

    a. If the nearest exit or stairwell is on fire or has another obstruction, go to the nearest unobstructed exit.

    b. If disabled students are in your classroom, evacuate them to the nearest, safe area that is designated "handicapped rescue." One such area should be available on each floor of your school. The best evacuation procedure is to have professional rescue personnel evacuate disabled students unless they are not safe remaining in the nearest designated area or the school building. You should have a plan to help disabled students to the next nearest safe designated area or from the building.

    NOTE: Emergency evacuation procedures require planning. Make sure the primary evacuation route is visibly posted on the floor plan for your area of your school. Alternate routes for escape should be determined because the primary route is often blocked by fire or other obstacles.

2. DO NOT USE ELEVATORS. You may be stranded in an elevator during an evacuation emergency if the elevator that you are in loses power. Elevator shafts also make excellent flues for conducting smoke and gases created by a fire. In addition, rescue is more difficult from an elevator than from a stairwell or classroom.

3. If you and your students are trapped in your classroom by a fire, try to remember the following rules.

    a. Test all doors before opening them.

        i. If a door has a glass panel, check the hallway or the other side of the door for fire or other hazards.

        ii. If a door does not have a glass panel, feel the door before opening it. Do not open the door if it feels hot or if smoke is seeping around the edges. Test the door by quickly touching the knob or handle with the back of your hand. The metal knob or handle conducts heat faster than the door panel.

        If the door is cool, stand behind it, open it slightly, and glance out before deciding whether to go through the doorway. Put your foot against the back of the door to prevent it from opening because of pressure from hot gases. If there are flames on the other side of the door, flinging the door open wide could create a draft and cause the fire to surge lethally into your classroom.

    b. Close doors and windows as you evacuate. (These actions will help slow the spread of flames.)

        i. If possible, close all windows in your classroom before you and your students leave the classroom.

    ii. Close the door to your classroom or any room through which you may pass.

  c. Stay low (crawl if necessary).

    i. Smoke fills an area from the ceiling down. Breathing and visibility will be easier near the floor.

    ii. Try not to inhale the smoke. Put a handkerchief or cloth—wet if possible—over your mouth and nose as an improvised filter.

4. If the primary and secondary exits are blocked, then follow the procedure below.

  a. Try to reach a window, ledge, or roof area. If your classroom is on the ground level of the school building, jump out of the window to escape the fire. After you are out, close the window if doing so will not endanger you or your students.

  b. If you must break a window to get out, use a chair, stool, or other convenient object to break the glass. If an object is not available, kick out the glass. As a last resort, use your hands, but wrap something around them first. Shield your eyes. In addition, tell your students to stand away from the window and to shield their eyes.

  c. Knock out any jagged pieces of glass left in the window before climbing through the window frame.

  d. If there is no safe way down, wave and shout to attract attention and signal for help.

5. If your clothing catches fire, drop and roll on the ground or floor. Never run because running will fan the fire on your clothing. Rolling will smother the flames on your clothes. While you are rolling on the ground or floor, call for help.

  a. When you roll on the ground to extinguish the fire on your person, cross your arms over your chest so that your hands touch your shoulders. This position helps keep flames away from your face.

  b. When you roll, roll slowly.

  c. If possible, wrap yourself in a rug, blanket, or coat before you roll on the ground.

  d. Get emergency medical assistance.

6. If someone else's clothing catches fire, then follow the steps below.

  a. Get the person who is on fire onto the floor as quickly as possible—trip the person if necessary.

  b. Make sure that the person rolls slowly. If possible, wrap the person in a rug, blanket, or coat before the person rolls on the ground.

  c. If possible, throw water over the burning person.

    d. After the fire on the person is out, do not attempt to pull clothing from the person's skin.

    e. Get emergency medical assistance.

7. After you and your students are out of the building, make sure that you follow the steps below.

    a. Move away from entrances to the building.

    b. Inform the fire department or police of the fire if you have not done so already. In addition, tell the authorities if someone is still in the building.

    c. Do not re-enter the building for clothing, valuables, or other items.

8. Only re-enter the building when told by someone in authority (fire department or police) that you may enter the building.

APPENDIX D: A List of Some Pertinent Regulations and Standards

Regulations

29 CFR 1910: OCCUPATIONAL SAFETY AND HEALTH STANDARDS

29 CFR 1910.94: Ventilation

29 CFR 1910.95: Occupational Noise Exposure

29 CFR 1910.96: Licensable Quantities of Materials Producing Ionizing Radiation

29 CFR 1910.97: Electromagnetic Radiation and Protective Measures

29 CFR 1910.101–105: Compressed Gases

    29 CFR 1910.101: General Requirements

    29 CFR 1910.102–105: Specific Gases (C_2H_2, H_2, O_2, NO)

29 CFR 1910.132: Personal Protective Equipment

29 CFR 1910.133: Eye and Face Protection

29 CFR 1910.134: Respiratory Protection

29 CFR 1910.135: Head Protection

29 CFR 1910.136: Foot Protection

29 CFR 1910.141: Sanitation

29 CFR 1910.144: Safety Color Code for Marking Physical Hazards

29 CFR 1910.145: Specification for Accident Prevention Signs and Tags

29 CFR 1910.251–254: Welding, Cutting, and Brazing

29 CFR 1910.301–398: Electrical Safety

    29 CFR 1910.331–360: Safety-Related Work Practices

    29 CFR 1910.361–380: Safety-Related Maintenance Requirements

    29 CFR 1910.381–98: Safety Requirements for Special Equipment

29 CFR 1910.1200: Hazard Communication Standard; Employee Right-to-Know

10 CFR 0–199: NUCLEAR REGULATORY COMMISSION

10 CFR 20: NRC Basic Standards for Radiation Protection

10 CFR 200–1099: DEPARTMENT OF ENERGY

10 CFR 834: Radiation Protection of the Public and the Environment

40 CFR 1–799: ENVIRONMENTAL PROTECTION AGENCY

40 CFR 61: EPA Air Emission Standards for Radionuclides

40 CFR 141: EPA Interim Drinking Water Standards for Radionuclides

Standards

AMERICAN NATIONAL STANDARDS INSTITUTE

ANSI Z87.1-1989   Practice for Occupational and Educational Eye and Face Protection

ANSI Z136.1-1993   Laser Safety

ANSI Z136.2-1986   Optical Fiber Safety

ANSI Z136.3-1988   Safe Use Lasers in the Health Care Environment

ANSI Z535.4-1996   Safety Signs and Labels

NATIONAL FIRE PROTECTION ASSOCIATION

NFPA 45: Fire Protection for Laboratories Using Chemicals

NFPA 49: Hazardous Chemical Data

NFPA 51B: Fire Prevention in the Use of Cutting and Welding Processes

NFPA 70: The National Electrical Code—1999 Handbook

COMPRESSED GAS ASSOCIATION (more pertinent publications are listed individually)

C-1–15: Cylinder Series Publications

2: Recommendations for the Disposition of Unserviceable Compressed Gas Cylinders with Known Contents

4: American National Standard Method of Marking Portable Compressed Gas Containers to Identify the Material Contained

6: Standards for Visual Inspection of Steel Compressed Gas Cylinders

7: Guide to the Preparation of Precautionary Labeling and Marking of Compressed Gas Containers

10: Recommended Procedures for Changes of Gas Service for Compressed Gas Cylinders

E-1–7: Regulators and Hose Line Equipment Series

1: Standard Connections for Regulator Outlets, Torches, and Fitted Hose for Welding and Cutting Equipment

2: Standard for Gas Regulators for Welding and Cutting

G-1–12: Gases Series

> 1: Acetylene
>
> 3: Sulfur Dioxide
>
> 4: Oxygen
>
> 5: Hydrogen
>
> 6: Carbon Dioxide
>
> 12: Hydrogen Sulfide

P-1–15: Protection and Handling Series

> 1: Safe Handling of Compressed Gases in Containers
>
> 6: Standard Density Data, Atmospheric Gases, and Hydrogen
>
> 9: The Inert Gases Argon, Nitrogen, and Helium
>
> 12: Safe Handling of Cryogenic Liquids
>
> 14: Accident Prevention in Oxygen-Rich and Oxygen-Deficient Atmospheres

S-1–7: Pressure Relief Device Series

> 1: Pressure Relief Device Standards—Part 1—Cylinders for Compressed Gases
>
> 7: Method for Selecting Pressure Relief Devices for Compressed Gas Mixtures in Cylinders

SB-1–11: Safety Bulletin Series

> 2: Oxygen-Deficient Atmospheres
>
> 6: Nitrous Oxide Security and Control
>
> 10: Correct Labeling and Proper Fittings on Cylinders/Containers

V-1–7: Valve Connections Series

> 1: American National, Canadian, and CGA Standard for Compressed Gas Cylinder Valve Outlet and Inlet Connections
>
> 6: Standard Cryogenic Liquid Transfer Connections

AV-1–9: Audiovisuals

> 1: Safe Handling and Storage of Compressed Gases
>
> 5: Safe Handling of Liquefied Nitrogen and Argon
>
> 7: Characteristics and Safe Handling of Carbon Dioxide
>
> 8: Characteristics and Safe Handling of Cryogenic Liquid and Gaseous Oxygen

Appendix E: Code of Federal Regulations, Title 29, Volume 6, Part 1910, pages 489–503

(revised as of July 1, 1998 and is from the U.S. Government Printing Office via GPO Access) (CITE: 29CFR1910.1450)

TITLE 29—LABOR

CHAPTER XVII—OCCUPATIONAL SAFETY AND HEALTH ADMINISTRATION, DEPARTMENT OF LABOR (Continued)

PART 1910—OCCUPATIONAL SAFETY AND HEALTH STANDARDS (Continued)— Table of Contents

Subpart Z—Toxic and Hazardous Substances

Sec. 1910.1450 Occupational exposure to hazardous chemicals in laboratories.

(a) Scope and application. (1) This section shall apply to all employers engaged in the laboratory use of hazardous chemicals as defined below.

(2) Where this section applies, it shall supersede, for laboratories, the requirements of all other OSHA health standards in 29 CFR part 1910, subpart Z, except as follows:

(i) For any OSHA health standard, only the requirement to limit employee exposure to the specific permissible exposure limit shall apply for laboratories, unless that particular standard states otherwise or unless the conditions of paragraph (a)(2)(iii) of this section apply.

(ii) Prohibition of eye and skin contact where specified by any OSHA health standard shall be observed.

(iii) Where the action level (or in the absence of an action level, the permissible exposure limit) is routinely exceeded for an OSHA regulated substance with exposure monitoring and medical surveillance requirements, paragraphs (d) and (g)(1)(ii) of this section shall apply.

(3) This section shall not apply to:

(i) Uses of hazardous chemicals which do not meet the definition of laboratory use, and in such cases, the employer shall comply with the relevant standard in 29 CFR part 1910, subpart Z, even if such use occurs in a laboratory.

(ii) Laboratory uses of hazardous chemicals which provide no potential for employee exposure. Examples of such conditions might include:

(A) Procedures using chemically-impregnated test media such as Dip-and-Read tests where a reagent strip is dipped into the specimen to be tested and the results are interpreted by comparing the color reaction to a color chart supplied by the manufacturer of the test strip; and

(B) Commercially prepared kits such as those used in performing pregnancy tests in which all of the reagents needed to conduct the test are contained in the kit.

(b) Definitions—

Action level means a concentration designated in 29 CFR part 1910 for a specific substance, calculated as an eight (8)-hour time-weighted average, which initiates certain required activities such as exposure monitoring and medical surveillance.

Assistant Secretary means the Assistant Secretary of Labor for Occupational Safety and Health, U.S. Department of Labor, or designee.

Carcinogen (see select carcinogen).

Chemical Hygiene Officer means an employee who is designated by the employer, and who is qualified by training or experience, to provide technical guidance in the development and implementation of the provisions of the Chemical Hygiene Plan. This definition is not intended to place limitations on the position description or job classification that the designated indvidual shall hold within the employer's organizational structure.

Chemical Hygiene Plan means a written program developed and implemented by the employer which sets forth procedures, equipment, personal protective equipment and work practices that (i) are capable of protecting employees from the health hazards presented by hazardous chemicals used in that particular workplace and (ii) meets the requirements of paragraph (e) of this section.

Combustible liquid means any liquid having a flashpoint at or above 100 deg.F (37.8 deg.C), but below 200 deg.F (93.3 deg.C), except any mixture having components with flashpoints of 200 deg.F (93.3 deg.C), or higher, the total volume of which make up 99 percent or more of the total volume of the mixture.

Compressed gas means:

(i) A gas or mixture of gases having, in a container, an absolute pressure exceeding 40 psi at 70 deg.F (21.1 deg.C); or

(ii) A gas or mixture of gases having, in a container, an absolute pressure exceeding 104 psi at 130 deg.F (54.4 deg.C) regardless of the pressure at 70 deg.F (21.1 deg.C); or

(iii) A liquid having a vapor pressure exceeding 40 psi at 100 deg.F (37.8 deg.C) as determined by ASTM D-323-72.

Designated area means an area which may be used for work with "select carcinogens," reproductive toxins or substances which have a high degree of acute toxicity. A designated area may be the entire laboratory, an area of a laboratory or a device such as a laboratory hood.

Emergency means any occurrence such as, but not limited to, equipment failure, rupture of containers or failure of control equipment which results in an uncontrolled release of a hazardous chemical into the workplace.

Employee means an individual employed in a laboratory workplace who may be exposed to hazardous chemicals in the course of his or her assignments.

Explosive means a chemical that causes a sudden, almost instantaneous release of pressure, gas, and heat when subjected to sudden shock, pressure, or high temperature.

Flammable means a chemical that falls into one of the following categories:

(i) Aerosol, flammable means an aerosol that, when tested by the method described in 16 CFR 1500.45, yields a flame protection exceeding 18 inches at full valve opening, or a flashback (a flame extending back to the valve) at any degree of valve opening;

(ii) Gas, flammable means:

(A) A gas that, at ambient temperature and pressure, forms a flammable mixture with air at a concentration of 13 percent by volume or less; or

(B) A gas that, at ambient temperature and pressure, forms a range of flammable mixtures with air wider than 12 percent by volume, regardless of the lower limit.

(iii) Liquid, flammable means any liquid having a flashpoint below 100 deg.F (37.8 deg.C), except any mixture having components with flashpoints of 100 deg.F (37.8 deg.C) or higher, the total of which make up 99 percent or more of the total volume of the mixture.

(iv) Solid, flammable means a solid, other than a blasting agent or explosive as defined in Sec. 1910.109(a), that is liable to cause fire through friction, absorption of moisture, spontaneous chemical change, or retained heat from manufacturing or processing, or which can be ignited readily and when ignited burns so vigorously and persistently as to create a serious hazard. A chemical shall be considered to be a flammable solid if, when tested by the method described in 16 CFR 1500.44, it ignites and burns with a self-sustained flame at a rate greater than one-tenth of an inch per second along its major axis.

Flashpoint means the minimum temperature at which a liquid gives off a vapor in sufficient concentration to ignite when tested as follows:

(i) Tagliabue Closed Tester (See American National Standard Method of Test for Flash Point by Tag Closed Tester, Z11.24-1979 (ASTM D 56-79))—for liquids with a viscosity of less than 45 Saybolt Universal Seconds (SUS) at 100 deg.F (37.8 deg.C), that do not contain suspended solids and do not have a tendency to form a surface film under test; or

(ii) Pensky-Martens Closed Tester (see American National Standard Method of Test for Flash Point by Pensky-Martens Closed Tester, Z11.7-1979 (ASTM D 93-79))—for liquids with a viscosity equal to or greater than 45 SUS at 100 deg.F (37.8 deg.C), or that contain suspended solids, or that have a tendency to form a surface film under test; or

(iii) Setaflash Closed Tester (see American National Standard Method of Test for Flash Point by Setaflash Closed Tester (ASTM D 3278-78)).

Organic peroxides, which undergo autoaccelerating thermal decomposition, are excluded from any of the flashpoint determination methods specified above.

Hazardous chemical means a chemical for which there is statistically significant evidence based on at least one study conducted in accordance with established scientific principles that acute or chronic health effects may occur in exposed employees. The term health hazard includes chemicals which are carcinogens, toxic or highly toxic agents, reproductive toxins, irritants, corrosives, sensitizers, hepatotoxins, nephrotoxins, neurotoxins, agents which act on the hematopoietic systems, and agents which damage the lungs, skin, eyes, or mucous membranes.

Appendices A and B of the Hazard Communication Standard (29 CFR 1910.1200) provide further guidance in defining the scope of health hazards and determining whether or not a chemical is to be considered hazardous for purposes of this standard.

Laboratory means a facility where the "laboratory use of hazardous chemicals" occurs. It is a workplace where relatively small quantities of hazardous chemicals are used on a non-production basis.

Laboratory scale means work with substances in which the containers used for reactions, transfers, and other handling of substances are designed to be easily and safely manipulated by one person. "Laboratory scale" excludes those workplaces whose function is to produce commercial quantities of materials.

Laboratory-type hood means a device located in a laboratory, enclosure on five sides with a moveable sash or fixed partial enclosed on the remaining side; constructed and maintained to draw air from the laboratory and to prevent or minimize the escape of air contaminants into the laboratory; and allows chemical manipulations to be conducted in the enclosure without insertion of any portion of the employee's body other than hands and arms.

Walk-in hoods with adjustable sashes meet the above definition provided that the sashes are adjusted during use so that the airflow and the exhaust of air contaminants are not compromised and employees do not work inside the enclosure during the release of airborne hazardous chemicals.

Laboratory use of hazardous chemicals means handling or use of such chemicals in which all of the following conditions are met:

(i) Chemical manipulations are carried out on a "laboratory scale;"

(ii) Multiple chemical procedures or chemicals are used;

(iii) The procedures involved are not part of a production process, nor in any way simulate a production process; and

(iv) "Protective laboratory practices and equipment" are available and in common use to minimize the potential for employee exposure to hazardous chemicals.

Medical consultation means a consultation which takes place between an employee and a licensed physician for the purpose of determining what medical examinations or procedures, if any, are appropriate in cases where a significant exposure to a hazardous chemical may have taken place.

Organic peroxide means an organic compound that contains the bivalent -O-O- structure and which may be considered to be a structural derivative of hydrogen peroxide where one or both of the hydrogen atoms has been replaced by an organic radical.

Oxidizer means a chemical other than a blasting agent or explosive as defined in Sec. 1910.109(a), that initiates or promotes combustion in other materials, thereby causing fire either of itself or through the release of oxygen or other gases.

Physical hazard means a chemical for which there is scientifically valid evidence that it is a combustible liquid, a compressed gas, explosive, flammable, an organic peroxide, an oxidizer, pyrophoric, unstable (reactive) or water-reactive.

Protective laboratory practices and equipment means those laboratory procedures, practices and equipment accepted by laboratory health and safety experts as effective, or that the employer can show to be effective, in minimizing the potential for employee exposure to hazardous chemicals.

Reproductive toxins means chemicals which affect the reproductive capabilities including chromosomal damage (mutations) and effects on fetuses (teratogenesis)

Select carcinogen means any substance which meets one of the following criteria:

(i) It is regulated by OSHA as a carcinogen; or

(ii) It is listed under the category, "known to be carcinogens," in the Annual Report on Carcinogens published by the National Toxicology Program (NTP) (latest edition); or

(iii) It is listed under Group 1 ("carcinogenic to humans") by the International Agency for Research on Cancer Monographs (IARC) (latest editions); or

(iv) It is listed in either Group 2A or 2B by IARC or under the category, "reasonably anticipated to be carcinogens" by NTP, and causes statistically significant tumor incidence in experimental animals in accordance with any of the following criteria:

(A) After inhalation exposure of 6–7 hours per day, 5 days per week, for a significant portion of a lifetime to dosages of less than 10 mg/m^3;

(B) After repeated skin application of less than 300 (mg/kg of body weight) per week; or

(C) After oral dosages of less than 50 mg/kg of body weight per day.

Unstable (reactive) means a chemical which is the pure state, or as produced or transported, will vigorously polymerize, decompose, condense, or will become self-reactive under conditions of shocks, pressure or temperature.

Water-reactive means a chemical that reacts with water to release a gas that is either flammable or presents a health hazard.

(c) Permissible exposure limits. For laboratory uses of OSHA regulated substances, the employer shall assure that laboratory employees' exposures to such substances do not exceed the permissible exposure limits specified in 29 CFR part 1910, subpart Z.

(d) Employee exposure determination—(1) Initial monitoring. The employer shall measure the employee's exposure to any substance regulated by a standard which requires monitoring if there is reason to believe that exposure levels for that substance routinely exceed the action level (or in the absence of an action level, the PEL).

(2) Periodic monitoring. If the initial monitoring prescribed by paragraph (d)(1) of this section discloses employee exposure over the action level (or in the absence of an action level, the PEL), the employer shall immediately comply with the exposure monitoring provisions of the relevant standard.

(3) Termination of monitoring. Monitoring may be terminated in accordance with the relevant standard.

(4) Employee notification of monitoring results. The employer shall, within 15 working days after the receipt of any monitoring results, notify the employee of these results in writing either individually or by posting results in an appropriate location that is accessible to employees.

(e) Chemical hygiene plan—General. (Appendix A of this section is non-mandatory but provides guidance to assist employers in the development of the Chemical Hygiene Plan.)

(1) Where hazardous chemicals as defined by this standard are used in the workplace, the employer shall develop and carry out the provisions of a written Chemical Hygiene Plan which is:

(i) Capable of protecting employees from health hazards associated with hazardous chemicals in that laboratory and

(ii) Capable of keeping exposures below the limits specified in paragraph (c) of this section.

(2) The Chemical Hygiene Plan shall be readily available to employees, employee representatives and, upon request, to the Assistant Secretary.

(3) The Chemical Hygiene Plan shall include each of the following elements and shall indicate specific measures that the employer will take to ensure laboratory employee protection:

(i) Standard operating procedures relevant to safety and health considerations to be followed when laboratory work involves the use of hazardous chemicals;

(ii) Criteria that the employer will use to determine and implement control measures to reduce employee exposure to hazardous chemicals including engineering controls, the use of personal protective equipment and hygiene practices; particular attention shall be given to the selection of control measures for chemicals that are known to be extremely hazardous;

(iii) A requirement that fume hoods and other protective equipment are functioning properly and specific measures that shall be taken to ensure proper and adequate performance of such equipment;

(iv) Provisions for employee information and training as prescribed in paragraph (f) of this section;

(v) The circumstances under which a particular laboratory operation, procedure or activity shall require prior approval from the employer or the employer's designee before implementation;

(vi) Provisions for medical consultation and medical examinations in accordance with paragraph (g) of this section;

(vii) Designation of personnel responsible for implementation of the Chemical Hygiene Plan including the assignment of a Chemical Hygiene Officer and, if appropriate, establishment of a Chemical Hygiene Committee; and

(viii) Provisions for additional employee protection for work with particularly hazardous substances. These include "select carcinogens," reproductive toxins and substances which have a high degree of acute toxicity. Specific consideration shall be given to the following provisions which shall be included where appropriate:

(A) Establishment of a designated area;

(B) Use of containment devices such as fume hoods or glove boxes;

(C) Procedures for safe removal of contaminated waste; and

(D) Decontamination procedures.

(4) The employer shall review and evaluate the effectiveness of the Chemical Hygiene Plan at least annually and update it as necessary.

(f) Employee information and training. (1) The employer shall provide employees with information and training to ensure that they are apprised of the hazards of chemicals present in their work area.

(2) Such information shall be provided at the time of an employee's initial assignment to a work area where hazardous chemicals are present and prior to assignments involving new exposure situations. The frequency of refresher information and training shall be determined by the employer.

(3) Information. Employees shall be informed of:

(i) The contents of this standard and its appendices which shall be made available to employees;

(ii) The location and availability of the employer's Chemical Hygiene Plan;

(iii) The permissible exposure limits for OSHA regulated substances or recommended exposure limits for other hazardous chemicals where there is no applicable OSHA standard;

(iv) Signs and symptoms associated with exposures to hazardous chemicals used in the laboratory; and

(v) The location and availability of known reference material on the hazards, safe handling, storage and disposal of hazardous chemicals found in the laboratory including, but not limited to, Material Safety Data Sheets received from the chemical supplier.

(4) Training. (i) Employee training shall include:

(A) Methods and observations that may be used to detect the presence or release of a hazardous chemical (such as monitoring conducted by the employer, continuous monitoring devices, visual appearance or odor of hazardous chemicals when being released, etc.);

(B) The physical and health hazards of chemicals in the work area; and

(C) The measures employees can take to protect themselves from these hazards, including specific procedures the employer has implemented to protect employees from exposure to hazardous chemicals, such as appropriate work practices, emergency procedures, and personal protective equipment to be used.

(ii) The employee shall be trained on the applicable details of the employer's written Chemical Hygiene Plan.

(g) Medical consultation and medical examinations. (1) The employer shall provide all employees who work with hazardous chemicals an opportunity to receive medical attention, including any follow-up examinations which the examining physician determines to be necessary, under the following circumstances:

(i) Whenever an employee develops signs or symptoms associated with a hazardous chemical to which the employee may have been exposed in the laboratory, the employee shall be provided an opportunity to receive an appropriate medical examination.

(ii) Where exposure monitoring reveals an exposure level routinely above the action level (or in the absence of an action level, the PEL) for an OSHA regulated substance for which there are exposure monitoring and medical surveillance requirements, medical surveillance shall be established for the affected employee as prescribed by the particular standard.

(iii) Whenever an event takes place in the work area such as a spill, leak, explosion or other occurrence resulting in the likelihood of a hazardous exposure, the affected employee shall be provided an opportunity for a medical consultation. Such consultation shall be for the purpose of determining the need for a medical examination.

(2) All medical examinations and consultations shall be performed by or under the direct supervision of a licensed physician and shall be provided without cost to the employee, without loss of pay and at a reasonable time and place.

(3) Information provided to the physician. The employer shall provide the following information to the physician:

(i) The identity of the hazardous chemical(s) to which the employee may have been exposed;

(ii) A description of the conditions under which the exposure occurred including quantitative exposure data, if available; and

(iii) A description of the signs and symptoms of exposure that the employee is experiencing, if any.

(4) Physician's written opinion. (i) For examination or consultation required under this standard, the employer shall obtain a written opinion from the examining physician which shall include the following:

(A) Any recommendation for further medical follow-up;

(B) The results of the medical examination and any associated tests;

(C) Any medical condition which may be revealed in the course of the examination which may place the employee at increased risk as a result of exposure to a hazardous chemical found in the workplace; and

(D) A statement that the employee has been informed by the physician of the results of the consultation or medical examination and any medical condition that may require further examination or treatment.

(ii) The written opinion shall not reveal specific findings of diagnoses unrelated to occupational exposure.

(h) Hazard identification. (1) With respect to labels and material safety data sheets:

(i) Employers shall ensure that labels on incoming containers of hazardous chemicals are not removed or defaced.

(ii) Employers shall maintain any material safety data sheets that are received with incoming shipments of hazardous chemicals, and ensure that they are readily accessible to laboratory employees.

(2) The following provisions shall apply to chemical substances developed in the laboratory:

(i) If the composition of the chemical substance which is produced exclusively for the laboratory's use is known, the employer shall determine if it is a hazardous chemical as defined in paragraph (b) of this section. If the chemical is determined to be hazardous, the employer shall provide appropriate training as required under paragraph (f) of this section.

(ii) If the chemical produced is a byproduct whose composition is not known, the employer shall assume that the substance is hazardous and shall implement paragraph (e) of this section.

(iii) If the chemical substance is produced for another user outside of the laboratory, the employer shall comply with the Hazard Communication Standard (29 CFR 1910.1200) including the requirements for preparation of material safety data sheets and labeling.

(i) Use of respirators. Where the use of respirators is necessary to maintain exposure below permissible exposure limits, the employer shall provide, at no cost to the employee, the proper respiratory equipment. Respirators shall be selected and used in accordance with the requirements of 29 CFR 1910.134.

(j) Recordkeeping. (1) The employer shall establish and maintain for each employee an accurate record of any measurements taken to monitor employee exposures and any medical consultation and examinations including tests or written opinions required by this standard.

(2) The employer shall assure that such records are kept, transferred, and made available in accordance with 29 CFR 1910.20.

(k) Dates—(1) Effective date. This section shall become effective May 1, 1990.

(2) Start-up dates. (i) Employers shall have developed and implemented a written Chemical Hygiene Plan no later than January 31, 1991.

(ii) Paragraph (a)(2) of this section shall not take effect until the employer has developed and implemented a written Chemical Hygiene Plan.

(l) Appendices. The information contained in the appendices is not intended, by itself, to create any additional obligations not otherwise imposed or to detract from any existing obligation.
[55 FR 3327, Jan. 31, 1990, 55 FR 7967, Mar. 6, 1990, 55 FR 12111, Mar. 30, 1990]

Appendix A to Sec. 1910.1450—National Research Council Recommendations

Concerning Chemical Hygiene in Laboratories (Non-Mandatory)
Table of Contents

Foreword

Corresponding Sections of the Standard and This Appendix

A. General Principles

1. Minimize all Chemical Exposures
2. Avoid Underestimation of Risk
3. Provide Adequate Ventilation
4. Institute a Chemical Hygiene Program
5. Observe the PELs and TLVs

B. Responsibilities

1. Chief Executive Officer
2. Supervisor of Administrative Unit
3. Chemical Hygiene Officer
4. Laboratory Supervisor
5. Project Director
6. Laboratory Worker

C. The Laboratory Facility

1. Design
2. Maintenance
3. Usage
4. Ventilation

D. Components of the Chemical Hygiene Plan

1. Basic Rules and Procedures
2. Chemical Procurement, Distribution, and Storage
3. Environmental Monitoring
4. Housekeeping, Maintenance and Inspections
5. Medical Program
6. Personal Protective Apparel and Equipment
7. Records
8. Signs and Labels
9. Spills and Accidents
10. Training and Information
11. Waste Disposal

E. General Procedures for Working With Chemicals

1. General Rules for all Laboratory Work with Chemicals
2. Allergens and Embryotoxins
3. Chemicals of Moderate Chronic or High Acute Toxicity
4. Chemicals of High Chronic Toxicity
5. Animal Work with Chemicals of High Chronic Toxicity

F. Safety Recommendations

G. Material Safety Data Sheets

Foreword

As guidance for each employer's development of an appropriate laboratory Chemical Hygiene Plan, the following non-mandatory recommendations are provided. They were extracted from "Prudent Practices for Handling Hazardous Chemicals in Laboratories" (referred to below as "Prudent Practices"), which was published in 1981 by the National Research Council and is available from the National Academy Press, 2101 Constitution Ave., NW., Washington DC 20418.

"Prudent Practices" is cited because of its wide distribution and acceptance and because of its preparation by members of the laboratory community through the sponsorship of the National Research Council. However, none of the recommendations given here will modify any requirements of the laboratory standard. This Appendix merely presents pertinent recommendations from "Prudent Practices", organized into a form convenient for quick reference during operation of a laboratory facility and during development and application of a Chemical Hygiene Plan. Users of this appendix should consult "Prudent Practices" for a more extended presentation and justification for each recommendation.

"Prudent Practices" deals with both safety and chemical hazards while the laboratory standard is concerned primarily with chemical hazards. Therefore, only those recommendations directed primarily toward control of toxic exposures are cited in this appendix, with the term "chemical hygiene" being substituted for the word "safety". However, since conditions producing or threatening physical injury often pose toxic risks as well, page references concerning major categories of safety hazards in the laboratory are given in section F.

The recommendations from "Prudent Practices" have been paraphrased, combined, or otherwise reorganized, and headings have been added. However, their sense has not been changed.

Corresponding Sections of the Standard and this Appendix

The following table is given for the convenience of those who are developing a Chemical Hygiene Plan which will satisfy the requirements of paragraph (e) of the standard. It indicates those sections of this appendix which are most pertinent to each of the sections of paragraph (e) and related paragraphs.

Paragraph and topic in laboratory standard Relevant appendix section		
(e)(3)(i)	Standard operating procedures for handling toxic chemicals.	C, D, E
(e)(3)(ii)	Criteria to be used for implementation of measures to reduce exposures.	D
(e)(3)(iii)	Fume hood performance	C4b
(e)(3)(iv)	Employee information and training (including emergency procedures).	D10, D9
(e)(3)(v)	Requirements for prior approval of laboratory activities.	E2b, E4b
(e)(3)(vi)	Medical consultation and medical examinations.	D5, E4f
(e)(3)(vii)	Chemical hygiene responsibilities	B
(e)(3)(viii)	Special precautions for work with particularly hazardous substances.	E2, E3, E4

In this appendix, those recommendations directed primarily at administrators and supervisors are given in sections A–D. Those recommendations of primary concern to employees who are actually handling laboratory chemicals are given in section E. (Reference to page numbers in "Prudent Practices" are given in parentheses.)

A. General Principles for Work with Laboratory Chemicals

In addition to the more detailed recommendations listed below in sections B–E, "Prudent Practices" expresses certain general principles, including the following:

1. It is prudent to minimize all chemical exposures. Because few laboratory chemicals are without hazards, general precautions for handling all laboratory chemicals should be adopted, rather than specific guidelines for particular chemicals (2, 10). Skin contact with chemicals should be avoided as a cardinal rule (198).

2. Avoid underestimation of risk. Even for substances of no known significant hazard, exposure should be minimized; for work with substances which present special hazards, special precautions should be taken (10, 37, 38). One should assume that any mixture will be more toxic than its most toxic component (30, 103) and that all substances of unknown toxicity are toxic (3, 34).

3. Provide adequate ventilation. The best way to prevent exposure to airborne substances is to prevent their escape into the working atmosphere by use of hoods and other ventilation devices (32, 198).

4. Institute a chemical hygiene program. A mandatory chemical hygiene program designed to minimize exposures is needed; it should be a regular, continuing effort, not merely a standby or short-term activity (6, 11). Its recommendations should be followed in academic teaching laboratories as well as by full-time laboratory workers (13).

5. Observe the PELs, TLVs. The Permissible Exposure Limits of OSHA and the Threshold Limit Values of the American Conference of Governmental Industrial Hygienists should not be exceeded (13).

B. Chemical Hygiene Responsibilities

Responsibility for chemical hygiene rests at all levels (6, 11, 21) including the:

1. Chief executive officer, who has ultimate responsibility for chemical hygiene within the institution and must, with other administrators, provide continuing support for institutional chemical hygiene (7, 11).

2. Supervisor of the department or other administrative unit, who is responsible for chemical hygiene in that unit (7).

3. Chemical hygiene officer(s), whose appointment is essential (7) and who must:

   (a) Work with administrators and other employees to develop and implement appropriate chemical hygiene policies and practices (7);

   (b) Monitor procurement, use, and disposal of chemicals used in the lab (8);

   (c) See that appropriate audits are maintained (8);

   (d) Help project directors develop precautions and adequate facilities (10);

   (e) Know the current legal requirements concerning regulated substances (50); and

(f) Seek ways to improve the chemical hygiene program (8, 11).

4. Laboratory supervisor, who has overall responsibility for chemical hygiene in the laboratory (21) including responsibility to:

(a) Ensure that workers know and follow the chemical hygiene rules, that protective equipment is available and in working order, and that appropriate training has been provided (21, 22);

(b) Provide regular, formal chemical hygiene and housekeeping inspections including routine inspections of emergency equipment (21, 171);

(c) Know the current legal requirements concerning regulated substances (50, 231);

(d) Determine the required levels of protective apparel and equipment (156, 160, 162); and

(e) Ensure that facilities and training for use of any material being ordered are adequate (215).

5. Project director or director of other specific operation, who has primary responsibility for chemical hygiene procedures for that operation (7).

6. Laboratory worker, who is responsible for:

(a) Planning and conducting each operation in accordance with the institutional chemical hygiene procedures (7, 21, 22, 230); and

(b) Developing good personal chemical hygiene habits (22).

C. The Laboratory Facility

1. **Design.** The laboratory facility should have:

(a) An appropriate general ventilation system (see C4 below) with air intakes and exhausts located so as to avoid intake of contaminated air (194);

(b) Adequate, well-ventilated stockrooms/storerooms (218, 219);

(c) Laboratory hoods and sinks (12, 162);

(d) Other safety equipment including eyewash fountains and drench showers (162, 169); and

(e) Arrangements for waste disposal (12, 240).

2. **Maintenance.** Chemical-hygiene-related equipment (hoods, incinerator, etc.) should undergo continuing appraisal and be modified if inadequate (11, 12).

3. **Usage.** The work conducted (10) and its scale (12) must be appropriate to the physical facilities available and, especially, to the quality of ventilation (13).

4. **Ventilation:**

(a) General laboratory ventilation. This system should: Provide a source of air for breathing and for input to local ventilation devices (199); it should not be relied on for protection from toxic substances released into the laboratory (198); ensure that laboratory air is continually replaced, preventing increase of air concentrations of toxic substances during the working day (194); direct air flow into the laboratory from non-laboratory areas and out to the exterior of the building (194).

(b) Hoods. A laboratory hood with 2.5 linear feet of hood space per person should be provided for every 2 workers if they spend most of their time working with chemicals (199); each hood should have a continuous monitoring device to allow convenient confirmation of adequate hood performance before use (200, 209). If this is not possible, work with substances of unknown toxicity should be avoided (13) or other types of local ventilation devices should be provided (199). See pp. 201–206 for a discussion of hood design, construction, and evaluation.

(c) Other local ventilation devices. Ventilated storage cabinets, canopy hoods, snorkels, etc. should be provided as needed (199). Each canopy hood and snorkel should have a separate exhaust duct (207).

(d) Special ventilation areas. Exhaust air from glove boxes and isolation rooms should be passed through scrubbers or other treatment before release into the regular exhaust system (208). Cold rooms and warm rooms should have provisions for rapid escape and for escape in the event of electrical failure (209).

(e) Modifications. Any alteration of the ventilation system should be made only if thorough testing indicates that worker protection from airborne toxic substances will continue to be adequate (12, 193, 204).

(f) Performance. Rate: 4–12 room air changes/hour is normally adequate general ventilation if local exhaust systems such as hoods are used as the primary method of control (194).

(g) Quality. General air flow should not be turbulent and should be relatively uniform throughout the laboratory, with no high velocity or static areas (194, 195); airflow into and within the hood should not be excessively turbulent (200); hood face velocity should be adequate (typically 60–100 lfm) (200, 204).

(h) Evaluation. Quality and quantity of ventilation should be evaluated on installation (202), regularly monitored (at least every 3 months) (6, 12, 14, 195), and reevaluated whenever a change in local ventilation devices is made (12, 195, 207). See pp. 195–198 for methods of evaluation and for calculation of estimated airborne contaminant concentrations.

D. Components of the Chemical Hygiene Plan

1. Basic Rules and Procedures (Recommendations for these are given in section E, below)

2. Chemical Procurement, Distribution, and Storage
   (a) Procurement. Before a substance is received, information on proper handling, storage, and disposal should be known to those who will be involved (215, 216). No container should be accepted without an adequate identifying label (216). Preferably, all substances should be received in a central location (216).
   (b) Stockrooms/storerooms. Toxic substances should be segregated in a well-identified area with local exhaust ventilation (221). Chemicals which are highly toxic (227) or other chemicals whose containers have been opened should be in unbreakable secondary containers (219). Stored chemicals should be examined periodically (at least annually) for replacement, deterioration, and container integrity (218–19). Stockrooms/storerooms should not be used as preparation or repackaging areas, should be open during normal working hours, and should be controlled by one person (219).
   (c) Distribution. When chemicals are hand carried, the container should be placed in an outside container or bucket. Freight-only elevators should be used if possible (223).
   (d) Laboratory storage. Amounts permitted should be as small as practical. Storage on bench tops and in hoods is inadvisable. Exposure to heat or direct sunlight should be avoided. Periodic inventories should be conducted, with unneeded items being discarded or returned to the storeroom/stockroom (225–6, 229).

3. Environmental Monitoring
   Regular instrumental monitoring of airborne concentrations is not usually justified or practical in laboratories but may be appropriate when testing or redesigning hoods or other ventilation devices (12) or when a highly toxic substance is stored or used regularly (e.g., 3 times/week) (13).

4. Housekeeping, Maintenance, and Inspections
   (a) Cleaning. Floors should be cleaned regularly (24).
   (b) Inspections. Formal housekeeping and chemical hygiene inspections should be held at least quarterly (6, 21) for units which have frequent pesonnel changes and semiannually for others; informal inspections should be continual (21).
   (c) Maintenance. Eye wash fountains should be inspected at intervals of not less than 3 months (6). Respirators for routine use should be inspected periodically by the laboratory supervisor (169). Safety showers should be tested routinely (169). Other safety equipment should be inspected regularly. (e.g., every 3–6 months) (6, 24, 171). Procedures to prevent restarting of out-of-service equipment should be established (25).

(d) Passageways. Stairways and hallways should not be used as storage areas (24). Access to exits, emergency equipment, and utility controls should never be blocked (24).

5. Medical Program
   (a) **Compliance with regulations.** Regular medical surveillance should be established to the extent required by regulations (12).
   (b) **Routine surveillance.** Anyone whose work involves regular and frequent handling of toxicologically significant quantities of a chemical should consult a qualified physician to determine on an individual basis whether a regular schedule of medical surveillance is desirable (11, 50).
   (c) **First aid.** Personnel trained in first aid should be available during working hours and an emergency room with medical personnel should be nearby (173). See pp. 176–178 for description of some emergency first aid procedures.

6. Protective Apparel and Equipment
   These should include for each laboratory:
   (a) Protective apparel compatible with the required degree of protection for substances being handled (158–161);
   (b) An easily accessible drench-type safety shower (162, 169);
   (c) An eyewash fountain (162);
   (d) A fire extinguisher (162–164);
   (e) Respiratory protection (164–9), fire alarm and telephone for emergency use (162) should be available nearby; and
   (f) Other items designated by the laboratory supervisor (156, 160).

7. Records
   (a) Accident records should be written and retained (174).
   (b) Chemical Hygiene Plan records should document that the facilities and precautions were compatible with current knowledge and regulations (7).
   (c) Inventory and usage records for high-risk substances should be kept as specified in sections E3e below.
   (d) Medical records should be retained by the institution in accordance with the requirements of state and federal regulations (12).

8. Signs and Labels
   Prominent signs and labels of the following types should be posted:
   (a) Emergency telephone numbers of emergency personnel/facilities, supervisors, and laboratory workers (28);
   (b) Identity labels, showing contents of containers (including waste receptacles) and associated hazards (27, 48);
   (c) Location signs for safety showers, eyewash stations, other safety and first aid equipment, exits (27) and areas where food and beverage consumption and storage are permitted (24); and

(**d**) Warnings at areas or equipment where special or unusual hazards exist (27).

9. Spills and Accidents

(**a**) A written emergency plan should be established and communicated to all personnel; it should include procedures for ventilation failure (200), evacuation, medical care, reporting, and drills (172).

(**b**) There should be an alarm system to alert people in all parts of the facility including isolation areas such as cold rooms (172).

(**c**) A spill control policy should be developed and should include consideration of prevention, containment, cleanup, and reporting (175).

(**d**) All accidents or near accidents should be carefully analyzed with the results distributed to all who might benefit (8, 28).

10. Information and Training Program

(**a**) **Aim:** To assure that all individuals at risk are adequately informed about the work in the laboratory, its risks, and what to do if an accident occurs (5, 15).

(**b**) **Emergency and Personal Protection Training:** Every laboratory worker should know the location and proper use of available protective apparel and equipment (154, 169).
Some of the full-time personnel of the laboratory should be trained in the proper use of emergency equipment and procedures (6).
Such training as well as first aid instruction should be available to (154) and encouraged for (176) everyone who might need it.

(**c**) Receiving and stockroom/storeroom personnel should know about hazards, handling equipment, protective apparel, and relevant regulations (217).

(**d**) **Frequency of Training:** The training and education program should be a regular, continuing activity—not simply an annual presentation (15).

(**e**) **Literature/Consultation:** Literature and consulting advice concerning chemical hygiene should be readily available to laboratory personnel, who should be encouraged to use these information resources (14).

11. Waste Disposal Program.

(**a**) **Aim:** To assure that minimal harm to people, other organisms, and the environment will result from the disposal of waste laboratory chemicals (5).

(**b**) **Content (14, 232, 233, 240):** The waste disposal program should specify how waste is to be collected, segregated, stored, and transported and include consideration of what materials can be incinerated. Transport from the institution must be in accordance with DOT regulations (244).

(c) **Discarding Chemical Stocks:** Unlabeled containers of chemicals and solutions should undergo prompt disposal; if partially used, they should not be opened (24, 27).

Before a worker's employment in the laboratory ends, chemicals for which that person was responsible should be discarded or returned to storage (226).

(d) **Frequency of Disposal:** Waste should be removed from laboratories to a central waste storage area at least once per week and from the central waste storage area at regular intervals (14).

(e) **Method of Disposal:** Incineration in an environmentally acceptable manner is the most practical disposal method for combustible laboratory waste (14, 238, 241).

Indiscriminate disposal by pouring waste chemicals down the drain (14, 231, 242) or adding them to mixed refuse for landfill burial is unacceptable (14).

Hoods should not be used as a means of disposal for volatile chemicals (40, 200).

Disposal by recycling (233, 243) or chemical decontamination (40, 230) should be used when possible.

E. Basic Rules and Procedures for Working with Chemicals

The Chemical Hygiene Plan should require that laboratory workers know and follow its rules and procedures. In addition to the procedures of the sub programs mentioned above, these should include the rules listed below.

1. General Rules
The following should be used for essentially all laboratory work with chemicals:

(a) **Accidents and spills**—Eye Contact: Promptly flush eyes with water for a prolonged period (15 minutes) and seek medical attention (33, 172).

Ingestion: Encourage the victim to drink large amounts of water (178).

Skin Contact: Promptly flush the affected area with water (33, 172, 178) and remove any contaminated clothing (172, 178). If symptoms persist after washing, seek medical attention (33).

Clean-up: Promptly clean up spills, using appropriate protective apparel and equipment and proper disposal (24, 33). See pp. 233–237 for specific clean-up recommendations.

(b) **Avoidance of "routine" exposure:** Develop and encourage safe habits (23); avoid unnecessary exposure to chemicals by any route (23);

Do not smell or taste chemicals (32). Vent apparatus which may discharge toxic chemicals (vacuum pumps, distillation columns, etc.) into local exhaust devices (199).
Inspect gloves (157) and test glove boxes (208) before use.
Do not allow release of toxic substances in cold rooms and warm rooms, since these have contained recirculated atmospheres (209).

(c) **Choice of chemicals:** Use only those chemicals for which the quality of the available ventilation system is appropriate (13).

(d) **Eating, smoking, etc.:** Avoid eating, drinking, smoking, gum chewing, or application of cosmetics in areas where laboratory chemicals are present (22, 24, 32, 40); wash hands before conducting these activities (23, 24).
Avoid storage, handling or consumption of food or beverages in storage areas, refrigerators, glassware or utensils which are also used for laboratory operations (23, 24, 226).

(e) **Equipment and glassware:** Handle and store laboratory glassware with care to avoid damage; do not use damaged glassware (25). Use extra care with Dewar flasks and other evacuated glass apparatus; shield or wrap them to contain chemicals and fragments should implosion occur (25). Use equipment only for its designed purpose (23, 26).

(f) **Exiting:** Wash areas of exposed skin well before leaving the laboratory (23).

(g) **Horseplay:** Avoid practical jokes or other behavior which might confuse, startle or distract another worker (23).

(h) **Mouth suction:** Do not use mouth suction for pipeting or starting a siphon (23, 32).

(i) **Personal apparel:** Confine long hair and loose clothing (23, 158). Wear shoes at all times in the laboratory but do not wear sandals, perforated shoes, or sneakers (158).

(j) **Personal housekeeping:** Keep the work area clean and uncluttered, with chemicals and equipment being properly labeled and stored; clean up the work area on completion of an operation or at the end of each day (24).

(k) **Personal protection:** Assure that appropriate eye protection (154-156) is worn by all persons, including visitors, where chemicals are stored or handled (22, 23, 33, 154).
Wear appropriate gloves when the potential for contact with toxic materials exists (157); inspect the gloves before each use, wash them before removal, and replace them periodically (157). (A table of resistance to chemicals of common glove materials is given p. 159).
Use appropriate (164–168) respiratory equipment when air contaminant concentrations are not sufficiently restricted by engineering controls (164–5), inspecting the respirator before use (169).

Use any other protective and emergency apparel and equipment as appropriate (22, 157–162).

Avoid use of contact lenses in the laboratory unless necessary; if they are used, inform supervisor so special precautions can be taken (155).

Remove laboratory coats immediately on significant contamination (161).

(l) **Planning:** Seek information and advice about hazards (7), plan appropriate protective procedures, and plan positioning of equipment before beginning any new operation (22, 23).

(m) **Unattended operations:** Leave lights on, place an appropriate sign on the door, and provide for containment of toxic substances in the event of failure of a utility service (such as cooling water) to an unattended operation (27, 128).

(n) **Use of hood:** Use the hood for operations which might result in release of toxic chemical vapors or dust (198–9).

As a rule of thumb, use a hood or other local ventilation device when working with any appreciably volatile substance with a TLV of less than 50 ppm (13).

Confirm adequate hood performance before use; keep hood closed at all times except when adjustments within the hood are being made (200); keep materials stored in hoods to a minimum and do not allow them to block vents or air flow (200).

Leave the hood "on" when it is not in active use if toxic substances are stored in it or if it is uncertain whether adequate general laboratory ventilation will be maintained when it is "off" (200).

(o) **Vigilance:** Be alert to unsafe conditions and see that they are corrected when detected (22).

(p) **Waste disposal:** Assure that the plan for each laboratory operation includes plans and training for waste disposal (230).

Deposit chemical waste in appropriately labeled receptacles and follow all other waste disposal procedures of the Chemical Hygiene Plan (22, 24).

Do not discharge to the sewer concentrated acids or bases (231); highly toxic, malodorous, or lachrymatory substances (231); or any substances which might interfere with the biological activity of waste water treatment plants, create fire or explosion hazards, cause structural damage or obstruct flow (242).

(q) **Working alone:** Avoid working alone in a building; do not work alone in a laboratory if the procedures being conducted are hazardous (28).

APPENDIX E

2. Working with Allergens and Embryotoxins
   (a) **Allergens (examples: diazomethane, isocyanates, bichromates):** Wear suitable gloves to prevent hand contact with allergens or substances of unknown allergenic activity (35).
   (b) **Embryotoxins (34–5) (examples: organomercurials, lead compounds, formamide):** If you are a woman of child-bearing age, handle these substances only in a hood whose satisfactory performance has been confirmed, using appropriate protective apparel (especially gloves) to prevent skin contact. Review each use of these materials with the research supervisor and review continuing uses annually or whenever a procedural change is made.
   Store these substances, properly labeled, in an adequately ventilated area in an unbreakable secondary container. Notify supervisors of all incidents of exposure or spills; consult a qualified physician when appropriate.

3. Work with Chemicals of Moderate Chronic or High Acute Toxicity
   Examples: diisopropylfluorophosphate (41), hydrofluoric acid (43), hydrogen cyanide (45).
   Supplemental rules to be followed in addition to those mentioned above (Procedure B of "Prudent Practices", pp. 39–41):
   (a) **Aim:** To minimize exposure to these toxic substances by any route using all reasonable precautions (39).
   (b) **Applicability:** These precautions are appropriate for substances with moderate chronic or high acute toxicity used in significant quantities (39).
   (c) **Location:** Use and store these substances only in areas of restricted access with special warning signs (40, 229).
   Always use a hood (previously evaluated to confirm adequate performance with a face velocity of at least 60 linear feet per minute) (40) or other containment device for procedures which may result in the generation of aerosols or vapors containing the substance (39); trap released vapors to prevent their discharge with the hood exhaust (40).
   (d) **Personal protection:** Always avoid skin contact by use of gloves and long sleeves (and other protective apparel as appropriate) (39).
   Always wash hands and arms immediately after working with these materials (40).
   (e) **Records:** Maintain records of the amounts of these materials on hand, amounts used, and the names of the workers involved (40, 229).
   (f) **Prevention of spills and accidents:** Be prepared for accidents and spills (41).

Assure that at least 2 people are present at all times if a compound in use is highly toxic or of unknown toxicity (39). Store breakable containers of these substances in chemically resistant trays; also work and mount apparatus above such trays or cover work and storage surfaces with removable, absorbent, plastic backed paper (40).

If a major spill occurs outside the hood, evacuate the area; assure that cleanup personnel wear suitable protective apparel and equipment (41).

(g) **Waste:** Thoroughly decontaminate or incinerate contaminated clothing or shoes (41). If possible, chemically decontaminate by chemical conversion (40).

Store contaminated waste in closed, suitably labeled, impervious containers (for liquids, in glass or plastic bottles half-filled with vermiculite) (40).

4. Work with Chemicals of High Chronic Toxicity

(Examples: dimethylmercury and nickel carbonyl (48), benzo-a-pyrene (51), N-nitrosodiethylamine (54), other human carcinogens or substances with high carcinogenic potency in animals (38).)

Further supplemental rules to be followed, in addition to all these mentioned above, for work with substances of known high chronic toxicity (in quantities above a few milligrams to a few grams, depending on the substance) (47). (Procedure A of "Prudent Practices" pp. 47–50).

(a) **Access:** Conduct all transfers and work with these substances in a "controlled area": a restricted access hood, glove box, or portion of a lab, designated for use of highly toxic substances, for which all people with access are aware of the substances being used and necessary precautions (48).

(b) **Approvals:** Prepare a plan for use and disposal of these materials and obtain the approval of the laboratory supervisor (48).

(c) **Non-contamination/Decontamination:** Protect vacuum pumps against contamination by scrubbers or HEPA filters and vent them into the hood (49). Decontaminate vacuum pumps or other contaminated equipment, including glassware, in the hood before removing them from the controlled area (49, 50).

Decontaminate the controlled area before normal work is resumed there (50).

(d) **Exiting:** On leaving a controlled area, remove any protective apparel (placing it in an appropriate, labeled container) and thoroughly wash hands, forearms, face, and neck (49).

(e) **Housekeeping:** Use a wet mop or a vacuum cleaner equipped with a HEPA filter instead of dry sweeping if the toxic substance was a dry powder (50).

(f) **Medical surveillance:** If using toxicologically significant quantities of such a substance on a regular basis (e.g., 3 times per week), consult a qualified physician concerning desirability of regular medical surveillance (50).

(g) **Records:** Keep accurate records of the amounts of these substances stored (229) and used, the dates of use, and names of users (48).

(h) **Signs and labels:** Assure that the controlled area is conspicuously marked with warning and restricted access signs (49) and that all containers of these substances are appropriately labeled with identity and warning labels (48).

(i) **Spills:** Assure that contingency plans, equipment, and materials to minimize exposures of people and property in case of accident are available (233–4).

(j) **Storage:** Store containers of these chemicals only in a ventilated, limited access (48, 227, 229) area in appropriately labeled, unbreakable, chemically resistant, secondary containers (48, 229).

(k) **Glove boxes:** For a negative pressure glove box, ventilation rate must be at least 2 volume changes/hour and pressure at least 0.5 inches of water (48). For a positive pressure glove box, thoroughly check for leaks before each use (49). In either case, trap the exit gases or filter them through a HEPA filter and then release them into the hood (49).

(l) **Waste:** Use chemical decontamination whenever possible; ensure that containers of contaminated waste (including washings from contaminated flasks) are transferred from the controlled area in a secondary container under the supervision of authorized personnel (49, 50, 233).

5. Animal Work with Chemicals of High Chronic Toxicity
   (a) **Access:** For large scale studies, special facilities with restricted access are preferable (56).
   (b) **Administration of the toxic substance:** When possible, administer the substance by injection or gavage instead of in the diet. If administration is in the diet, use a caging system under negative pressure or under laminar air flow directed toward HEPA filters (56).
   (c) **Aerosol suppression:** Devise procedures which minimize formation and dispersal of contaminated aerosols, including those from food, urine, and feces (e.g., use HEPA filtered vacuum equipment for cleaning, moisten contaminated bedding before removal from the cage, mix diets in closed containers in a hood) (55, 56).
   (d) **Personal protection:** When working in the animal room, wear plastic or rubber gloves, fully buttoned laboratory coat or jumpsuit and, if needed because of incomplete suppression

of aerosols, other apparel and equipment (shoe and head coverings, respirator) (56).

(e) **Waste disposal:** Dispose of contaminated animal tissues and excreta by incineration if the available incinerator can convert the contaminant to non-toxic products (238); otherwise, package the waste appropriately for burial in an EPA-approved site (239).

F. Safety Recommendations

The above recommendations from "Prudent Practices" do not include those which are directed primarily toward prevention of physical injury rather than toxic exposure. However, failure of precautions against injury will often have the secondary effect of causing toxic exposures. Therefore, we list below page references for recommendations concerning some of the major categories of safety hazards which also have implications for chemical hygiene:

1. Corrosive agents: (35–6)
2. Electrically powered laboratory apparatus: (179–92)
3. Fires, explosions: (26, 57–74, 162–4, 174–5, 219–20, 226–7)
4. Low temperature procedures: (26, 88)
5. Pressurized and vacuum operations (including use of compressed gas cylinders): (27, 75–101)

G. Material Safety Data Sheets

Material safety data sheets are presented in "Prudent Practices" for the chemicals listed below. (Asterisks denote that comprehensive material safety data sheets are provided).

* Acetyl peroxide (105)
* Acrolein (106)
* Acrylonitrile (107)
  Ammonia (anhydrous) (91)
* Aniline (109)
* Benzene (110)
* Benzo[a]pyrene (112)
* Bis(chloromethyl) ether (113)
  Boron trichloride (91)
  Boron trifluoride (92)
  Bromine (114)
* Tert-butyl hydroperoxide (148)
* Carbon disulfide (116)
  Carbon monoxide (92)
* Carbon tetrachloride (118)
* Chlorine (119)

Chlorine trifluoride (94)
* Chloroform (121)
Chloromethane (93)
* Diethyl ether (122)
Diisopropyl fluorophosphate (41)
* Dimethylformamide (123)
* Dimethyl sulfate (125)
* Dioxane (126)
* Ethylene dibromide (128)
* Fluorine (95)
* Formaldehyde (130)
* Hydrazine and salts (132)
Hydrofluoric acid (43)
Hydrogen bromide (98)
Hydrogen chloride (98)
* Hydrogen cyanide (133)
* Hydrogen sulfide (135)
Mercury and compounds (52)
* Methanol (137)
* Morpholine (138)
* Nickel carbonyl (99)
* Nitrobenzene (139)
Nitrogen dioxide (100)
N-nitrosodiethylamine (54)
* Peracetic acid (141)
* Phenol (142)
* Phosgene (143)
* Pyridine (144)
* Sodium azide (145)
* Sodium cyanide (147)
Sulfur dioxide (101)
* Trichloroethylene (149)
* Vinyl chloride (150)

Appendix B to Sec. 1910.1450—References (Non-Mandatory)

The following references are provided to assist the employer in the development of a Chemical Hygiene Plan. The materials listed below are offered as non-mandatory guidance. References listed here do not imply specific endorsement of a book, opinion, technique, policy or a specific solution for a safety or health problem. Other references not listed here may better meet the needs of a specific laboratory.

(a) Materials for the development of the Chemical Hygiene Plan:
1. American Chemical Society, Safety in Academic Chemistry Laboratories, 4th edition, 1985.

2. Fawcett, H.H. and W. S. Wood, Safety and Accident Prevention in Chemical Operations, 2nd edition, Wiley-Interscience, New York, 1982.

3. Flury, Patricia A., Environmental Health and Safety in the Hospital Laboratory, Charles C. Thomas Publisher, Springfield IL, 1978.

4. Green, Michael E. and Turk, Amos, Safety in Working with Chemicals, Macmillan Publishing Co., NY, 1978.

5. Kaufman, James A., Laboratory Safety Guidelines, Dow Chemical Co., Box 1713, Midland, MI 48640, 1977.

6. National Institutes of Health, NIH Guidelines for the Laboratory use of Chemical Carcinogens, NIH Pub. No. 81-2385, GPO, Washington, DC 20402, 1981.

7. National Research Council, Prudent Practices for Disposal of Chemicals from Laboratories, National Academy Press, Washington, DC, 1983.

8. National Research Council, Prudent Practices for Handling Hazardous Chemicals in Laboratories, National Academy Press, Washington, DC, 1981.

9. Renfrew, Malcolm, Ed., Safety in the Chemical Laboratory, Vol. IV, J. Chem. Ed., American Chemical Society, Easlon, PA, 1981.

10. Steere, Norman V., Ed., Safety in the Chemical Laboratory, J. Chem. Ed. American Chemical Society, Easlon, PA, 18042, Vol. I, 1967, Vol. II, 1971, Vol. III 1974.

11. Steere, Norman V., Handbook of Laboratory Safety, the Chemical Rubber Company Cleveland, OH, 1971.

12. Young, Jay A., Ed., Improving Safety in the Chemical Laboratory, John Wiley & Sons, Inc. New York, 1987.

(b) Hazardous Substances Information:

1. American Conference of Governmental Industrial Hygienists, Threshold Limit Values for Chemical Substances and Physical Agents in the Workroom Environment with Intended Changes, 6500 Glenway Avenue, Bldg. D-7 Cincinnati, OH 45211-4438 (latest edition).

2. Annual Report on Carcinogens, National Toxicology Program U.S. Department of Health and Human Services, Public Health Service, U.S. Government Printing Office, Washington, DC, (latest edition).

3. Best Company, Best Safety Directory, Vols. I and II, Oldwick, N.J., 1981.

4. Bretherick, L., Handbook of Reactive Chemical Hazards, 2nd edition, Butterworths, London, 1979.

5. Bretherick, L., Hazards in the Chemical Laboratory, 3rd edition, Royal Society of Chemistry, London, 1986.

6. Code of Federal Regulations, 29 CFR part 1910 subpart Z. U.S. Govt. Printing Office, Washington, DC 20402 (latest edition).

7. IARC Monographs on the Evaluation of the Carcinogenic Risk of Chemicals to Man, World Health Organization Publications Center, 49 Sheridan Avenue, Albany, New York 12210 (latest editions).

8. NIOSH/OSHA Pocket Guide to Chemical Hazards. NIOSH Pub. No. 85-114, U.S. Government Printing Office, Washington, DC, 1985 (or latest edition).

9. Occupational Health Guidelines, NIOSH/OSHA NIOSH Pub. No. 81-123 U.S. Government Printing Office, Washington, DC, 1981.

10. Patty, F.A., Industrial Hygiene and Toxicology, John Wiley & Sons, Inc., New York, NY (Five Volumes).

11. Registry of Toxic Effects of Chemical Substances, U.S. Department of Health and Human Services, Public Health Service, Centers for Disease Control, National Institute for Occupational Safety and Health, Revised Annually, for sale from Superintendent of Documents U.S. Govt. Printing Office, Washington, DC 20402.

12. The Merck Index: An Encyclopedia of Chemicals and Drugs. Merck and Company Inc. Rahway, N.J., 1976 (or latest edition).

13. Sax, N.I. Dangerous Properties of Industrial Materials, 5th edition, Van Nostrand Reinhold, NY., 1979.

14. Sittig, Marshall, Handbook of Toxic and Hazardous Chemicals, Noyes Publications, Park Ridge, NJ, 1981.

(c) Information on Ventilation:

1. American Conference of Governmental Industrial Hygienists Industrial Ventilation (latest edition), 6500 Glenway Avenue, Bldg. D-7, Cincinnati, Ohio 45211-4438.

2. American National Standards Institute, Inc. American National Standards Fundamentals Governing the Design and Operation of Local Exhaust Systems ANSI Z 9.2-1979 American National Standards Institute, N.Y. 1979.

3. Imad, A.P. and Watson, C.L. Ventilation Index: An Easy Way to Decide about Hazardous Liquids, Professional Safety pp. 15–18, April 1980.

4. National Fire Protection Association, Fire Protection for Laboratories Using Chemicals NFPA-45, 1982. Safety Standard for Laboratories in Health Related Institutions, NFPA, 56c, 1980. Fire Protection Guide on Hazardous Materials, 7th edition, 1978. National Fire Protection Association, Batterymarch Park, Quincy, MA 02269.

5 Scientific Apparatus Makers Association (SAMA), Standard for Laboratory Fume Hoods, SAMA LF7-1980, 1101 16th Street, NW., Washington, DC 20036.

(d) Information on Availability of Referenced Material:
1. American National Standards Institute (ANSI), 1430 Broadway, New York, NY 10018.
2. American Society for Testing and Materials (ASTM), 1916 Race Street, Philadelphia, PA 19103. [55 FR 3327, Jan. 31, 1990; 55 FR 7967, Mar. 6, 1990; 57 FR 29204, July 1, 1992; 61 FR 5508, Feb. 13, 1996]

Editorial Note: This listing is provided for information purposes only. It is compiled and kept up-to-date by the Department of Labor.

APPENDIX E

HOLT SCIENCE

Laboratory Manager's
Professional Reference

Understand risk management and the hazards that can occur in your classroom with this *Laboratory Manager's Professional Reference*. Also learn how to prevent or to eliminate each type of hazard by referring to this well-organized reference.

HOLT, RINEHART AND WINSTON

A Harcourt Education Company

ISBN 0-03-064921-8

90000

9 780030 649219